THE FUTURE OF DISTANCE LEARNING

THE FUTURE OF DISTANCE LEARNING

Editor

Prof. Ramesh Chandra

Publications

KALPAZ PUBLICATIONS

DELHI-110052

THE FUTURE OF DISTANCE LEARNING

The Future of Distance Learning

Rs. 850

ISBN: 81-7835-236-2

This book is Vol. No. 8 of Universal Education and Technology in 21st Century (Set)

Published in 2005 in India by
Kalpaz Publications,
C-30, Satyawati Nagar, Delhi-110052
E-mail : Kalpaz@hotmail.com

Laser Typesetting at : Master Computers, Delhi
Printed at : Ajit Printers, Delhi

Contents

Preface vii

1. **Distance Learning: The Millennium Concept** 1
Teaching Strategies; Learning Strategies.

2. **Web-Oriented Distance Learning** 26
Constructivism; Future of Net-Based Training; Building the Information Driveway.

3. **Development of Distance Learning** 53
The Design Stage; The Development Stage; The Evaluation Stage; The Revision Stage; Instructional Tools; Instructional Television; Interactive Videoconferencing; Types of Videoconferencing Systems; Designing Instruction for Interactive Video; Instructional Strategies; Computers in Distance Education; Internet and Distance Education; Print in Distance Education; Multimedia use in Instruction.

4. **Open Learning: An Analysis** 112
Internet and the Humanities.

5. **Open Learning Communities** 132
Concept of Open Learning Communities; Recontextualising Teachers' Role.

6. **Distance Learning and Copyright Issues** 196
Copyright Law and Promotion of Distance Education.

7. **The Future of Distance Learning** 254
Effect of Commercialization; Challenges of

Distance Learning; Accreditation of Distance Learning; Effectiveness of Distance Learning; Analytic Approach; Implications.

Bibliography 300

Index 302

Preface

The term 'distance education' refers to the process of learning in which there is spatial, and usually temporal, distance between the teacher and learner, on the other hand 'open education' refers to the process of making learning available to a learner at a place and time of his/her choice, and at a rate suitable to the learner.

Distance education in its earliest form utilised only the print media. Subsequently, in the period between the two World Wars projectors of different types and audio cassettes were added as teaching aids in traditional education and the latter made its entry in distance education also. A little later video films were added to the repertoire of teaching aids.

The years following World War II saw rapid developments in the field of communication technology opening up new pathways in both formal and non-formal education, and especially in the latter. The development of computer-based technologies has revolutionised teaching and learning process. The advent of virtual classrooms and video desktop promises interesting possibilities, including the re-merger of the formal and informal streams.

Distance learning environment is an evolving paradigm of instruction and learning that attempts to overcome both the distance and time constraints found in traditional classroom learning. The advantages of distance learning provides the learner a choice to continue education as a part-time and pastime activity at his own pace, place and time. There are no two opinions over the usefulness of this system to literate people faster and make higher education accessible to all.

Editor

1

Distance Learning: The Millennium Concept

Distance education takes place when a teacher and students are separated by physical distance, and technology, often in concert with face-to-face communication, is used to bridge the instructional gap. These types of programs can provide adults with a second chance at a college education, reach those disadvantaged by limited time, distance or physical disability, and update the knowledge base of workers at their places of employment. Research comparing distance education to traditional face-to-face instruction indicates that teaching and studying at a distance can be as effective as traditional instruction, when the method and technologies used are appropriate to the instructional tasks, there is student-to-student interaction, and when there is timely teacher-to- student feedback. A wide range of technological options are available to the distance educator. They fall into four major categories:

— *Voice* - Instructional audio tools include the interactive technologies of telephone, audioconferencing, and short-wave radio. Passive (i.e., one-way) audio tools include tapes and radio.

— *Video* - Instructional video tools include still images such as slides, pre-produced moving images (e.g., film, videotape), and real-time moving images combined with audioconferencing (one-way or two-way video with two-way audio).

— *Data* - Computers send and receive information electronically. For this reason, the term "data" is used to describe this broad category of instructional tools. Computer applications for distance education are varied and include:

  — *Computer-assisted instruction (CAI)* - uses the computer as a self-contained teaching machine to present individual lessons.

  — *Computer-managed instruction (CMI)* - uses the computer to organize instruction and track student records and progress. The instruction itself need not be delivered via a computer, although CAI is often combined with CMI.

  — *Computer-mediated education (CME)* - describes computer applications that facilitate the delivery of instruction. Examples include electronic mail, fax, real-time computer conferencing, and World-Wide Web applications.

— *Print* - is a foundational element of distance education programs and the basis from which all other delivery systems have evolved. Various print formats are available including: textbooks, study guides, workbooks, course syllabi, and case studies.

Alh technology plays a key role in the delivery of distance education, educators must remain focused on instructional outcomes, not the technology of delivery. The key to effective distance education is focusing on the needs of the learners, the requirements of the content, and the constraints faced by the teacher, before selecting a delivery system. Typically, this systematic approach will result in a mix of media, each serving a specific purpose. For example:

— A strong print component can provide much of the basic instructional content in the form of a course text, as well as readings, the syllabus, and day-to-day schedule.

— Interactive audio or video conferencing can provide real time face-to-face (or voice-to-voice) interaction. This is also an excellent and cost-effective way to incorporate guest speakers and content experts.

— Computer conferencing or electronic mail can be used to send messages, assignment feedback, and other targeted communication to one or more class members. It can also be used to increase interaction among students.

— Pre-recorded video tapes can be used to present class lectures and visually oriented content.

— Fax can be used to distribute assignments, last minute announcements, to receive student assignments, and to provide timely feedback.

Using this integrated approach, the educator's task is to carefully select among the technological options. The goal is to build a mix of instructional media, meeting the needs of the learner in a manner that is instructionally effective and economically prudent. Without exception, effective distance education programs begin with careful planning and a focused understanding of course requirements and student needs. Appropriate technology can only be selected once these elements are understood in detail.

There is no mystery to the way effective distance education programs develop. They don't happen spontaneously; they evolve through the hard work and dedicated efforts of many individuals and organizations. In fact, successful distance education programs rely on the consistent and integrated efforts of students, faculty, facilitators, support staff, and administrators.

The following briefly describes the roles of these key players in the distance education enterprise and the challenges they face.

— *Students* - Meeting the instructional needs of students is the cornerstone of every effective distance education program, and the test by which all efforts in the field are judged. Regardless of the educational context, the primary role of the student is to learn. This is a daunting task under the best of circumstances, requiring motivation, planning, and an ability to analyze and apply the instructional content being taught. When instruction is delivered at a distance, additional challenges result because students are often separated from others sharing their backgrounds and interests, have few if any opportunities to interact with teachers outside of class, and must rely on technical linkages to bridge the gap separating class participants.

— *Faculty* - The success of any distance education effort rests squarely on the shoulders of the faculty. In a traditional classroom setting, the instructor's responsibility includes assembling course content and developing an understanding of student needs.

Special challenges confront those teaching at a distance. For example, the instructor must:

— Develop an understanding of the characteristics and needs of distant students with little first-hand experience and limited, if any, face-to-face contact.

— Adapt teaching styles taking into consideration the needs and expectations of multiple, often diverse, audiences.

— Develop a working understanding of delivery technology, while remaining focused on their teaching role.

— Function effectively as a skilled facilitator as well as content provider.

— Facilitators - The instructor often finds it beneficial to rely on a site facilitator to act as a bridge between the students and the instructor. To be effective, a facilitator must understand the students being served and the instructor's expectations. Most importantly, the facilitator must be willing to follow the directive established by the teacher. Where budget and logistics permit, the role of on-site facilitators has increased even in classes in which they have little, if any, content expertise. At a minimum, they set up equipment, collect assignments, proctor tests, and act as the instructor's on-site eyes and ears.

— Support Staff - These individuals are the silent heroes of the distance education enterprise and ensure that the myriad details required for program success are dealt with effectively. Most successful distance education programs consolidate support service functions to include student registration, materials duplication and distribution, textbook ordering, securing of copyright clearances, facilities scheduling, processing grade reports, managing technical resources, etc.. Support personnel are truly the glue that keeps the distance education effort together and on track.

— Administrators - Although administrators are typically influential in planning an institution's distance education program, they often lose contact or relinquish control to technical managers once the program is operational. Effective distance education administrators are more than idea people. They are consensus builders, decision makers, and referees. They work closely with technical and support service personnel, ensuring that technological resources are effectively deployed to further the institution's academic mission. Most importantly, they maintain an academic focus, realizing that meeting the instructional needs of distant students is their ultimate responsibility.

Teaching Strategies

Classroom teachers rely on a number of visual and unobtrusive cues from their students to enhance their delivery of instructional content. A quick glance, for example, reveals who is attentively taking notes, pondering a difficult concept, or preparing to make a comment. The student who is frustrated, confused, tired, or bored is equally evident. The attentive teacher consciously and subconsciously receives and analyzes these visual cues and adjusts the course delivery to meet the needs of the class during a particular lesson. In contrast, the distant teacher has few, if any, visual cues. Those cues that do exist are filtered through technological devices such as video monitors. It is difficult to carry on a stimulating teacher-class discussion when spontaneity is altered by technical requirements and distance.

Without the use of a real-time visual medium such as television, the teacher receives no visual information from the distant sites. The teacher might never really know, for example, if students are asleep, talking among themselves or even in the room. Separation by distance also affects the general rapport of the class. Living in different communities, geographic regions, or even states deprives the teacher and students of a common community link.

Many teachers feel the opportunities offered by distance education outweigh the obstacles. In fact, instructors often comment that the focused preparation required by distance teaching improves their overall teaching and empathy for their students. The challenges posed by distance education are countered by opportunities to:

— Reach a wider student audience

— Meet the needs of students who are unable to attend on-campus classes

— Involve outside speakers who would otherwise be unavailable

— Link students from different social, cultural, economic, and experiential backgrounds

In developing or adapting distance instruction, the core content remains basically unchanged, although its presentation requires new strategies and additional preparation time. Suggestions for planning and organizing a distance delivered course include:

— Begin the course planning process by studying distance education research findings. There are several research summaries available.

— Before developing something new, check and review existing materials for content and presentation ideas.

— Analyze and understand the strengths and weaknesses of the possible delivery systems available to you (e.g., audio, video, data, and print) not only in terms of how they are delivered (e.g., satellite, microwave, fiber optic cable, etc..), but in terms of learner needs and course requirements before selecting a mix of instructional technology.

— Hands-on training with the technology of delivery is critical for both teacher and students. Consider a pre-class session in which the class meets informally using the delivery technology and learns about the roles and responsibilities of technical support staff.

— At the start of class initiate a frank discussion to set rules, guidelines, and standards. Once procedures have been established, consistently uphold them.

— Make sure each site is properly equipped with functional and accessible equipment. Provide a toll-free "hotline" for reporting and rectifying problems.

— If course materials are sent by mail, make sure they are received well before class begins. To help students keep materials organized, consider binding the syllabus, handouts, and other readings prior to distribution.

— Start off slowly with a manageable number of sites and students. The logistical difficulties of distant teaching increase with each additional site.

To function effectively, students must quickly become comfortable with the nature of teaching and learning at a distance. Efforts should be made to adapt the delivery system to best motivate and meet the needs of the students, in terms of both content and preferred learning styles. Consider the following strategies for meeting students' needs:

— Assist students in becoming both familiar and comfortable with the delivery technology and prepare them to resolve the technical problems that will arise. Focus on joint problem solving, not placing blame for the occasional technical difficulty.

— Make students aware of and comfortable with new patterns of communication to be used in the course.

— Learn about students' backgrounds and experiences. Discussing the instructor's background and interests is equally important.

— Be sensitive to different communication styles and varied cultural backgrounds. Remember, for example, that students may have different language skills, and that humor is culturally specific and won't be perceived the same way by all.

— Remember that students must take an active role in the distance delivered course by independently taking responsibility for their learning.

— Be aware of students' needs in meeting standard university deadlines, despite the lag time often involved in rural mail delivery.

For the most part, effective distance teaching requires the enhancement of existing skills, rather than developing new abilities. Pay special attention to the following:

— Realistically assess the amount of content that can be effectively delivered in the course. Because of the logistics involved, presenting content at a distance is usually more time consuming than presenting the same content in a traditional classroom.

— Be aware that student participants will have different learning styles. Some will learn easily in group settings, while others will excel when working independently.

— Diversify and pace course activities and avoid long lectures. Intersperse content presentations with discussions and student-centered exercises.

— Humanize the course by focusing on the students, not the delivery system.

— Consider using a print component to supplement non-print materials.

— Use locally relevant case studies and examples as often as possible to assist students in understanding and applying course content. Typically, the earlier in the course this is done, the better.

— Be concise. Use short, cohesive statements and ask direct questions, realizing that technical linkages might increase the time it takes for students to respond.

— Develop strategies for student reinforcement, review, repetition, and remediation. Towards this end, one-on-one phone discussions and electronic mail communication can be especially effective.

Using effective interaction and feedback strategies will enable the instructor to identify and meet individual student needs while providing a forum for suggesting course improvements. To improve interaction and feedback, consider the following:

— Use pre-class study questions and advance organizers to encourage critical thinking and informed participation on the part of all learners. Realize that it will take time to improve poor communication patterns.

— Early in the course, require students to contact you and interact among themselves via electronic mail, so they become comfortable with the process. Maintaining and sharing electronic journal entries can be very effective toward this end.

— Arrange telephone office hours using a toll-free number. Set evening office hours if most of your students work during the day.

— Integrate a variety of delivery systems for interaction and feedback, including one-on-one and conference calls, fax, E-mail, video, and computer conferencing. When feasible, consider personal visits as well.

— Contact each site (or student) every week if possible, especially early in the course. Take note of students who don't participate during the first session, and contact them individually after class.

— Use pre-stamped and addressed postcards, out-of-class phone conferences, and e-mail for feedback regarding course content, relevancy, pace, delivery problems, and instructional concerns.

— Have students keep a journal of their thoughts and ideas regarding the course content, as well as their individual progress and other concerns. Have students submit journal entries frequently.

— Use an on-site facilitator to stimulate interaction when distant students are hesitant to ask questions or participate. In addition, the facilitator can act as your on-site "eyes and ears".

— Call on individual students to ensure that all participants have ample opportunity to interact. At the same time, politely but firmly discourage individual students or sites from monopolizing class time.

— Make detailed comments on written assignments, referring to additional sources for supplementary information. Return assignments without delay, using fax or electronic mail, if practical.

Learning Strategies

In a distance education setting, the process of student learning is more complex for several reasons:

— Many distance-education students are older, have jobs, and families. They must coordinate the different areas of their lives which influence each other — their families, jobs, spare time, and studies.

— Distant students have a variety of reasons for taking courses. Some students are interested in obtaining a degree to qualify for a better job. Many take courses to broaden their education and are not really interested in completing a degree.

— In distance education, the learner is usually isolated. The motivational factors arising from the contact or competition with other students is absent. The student also lacks the immediate support of a teacher who is present and able to motivate and, if necessary, give attention to actual needs and difficulties that crop up during study.

— Distant students and their teachers often have little in common in terms of background and day-to-day experiences and therefore, it takes longer for student-teacher rapport to develop. Without face-to-face contact distant students may feel ill at ease with their teacher as an "individual" and uncomfortable with their learning situation.

— In distance education settings, technology is typically the conduit through which information and communication flow. Until the teacher and students become comfortable with the technical delivery system, communication will be inhibited.

Beginning students may have some difficulty determining what the demands of a course of academic study actually are because they do not have the support of an immediate peer group, ready access to the instructor, or familiarity with the technology being used for delivery of the distance-education course. They may be unsure of themselves and their learning. Morgan suggests that distant students who are not confident about their learning tend to concentrate on memorizing facts and details in order to complete assignments and write exams. As a result, they end up with a poor understanding of course material. He views memorization of facts and details as a "surface approach" to learning and summarizes it as follows:

— Surface approach:

— Focus on the "signs" such as the text or instruction itself.

— Focus on discrete elements.

— Memorize information and procedures for tests.

— Unreflectively associate concepts and facts.

— Fail to distinguish principles from evidence, new information from old.

— Treat assignments as something imposed by the instructor.

— External emphasis focusing on the demands of assignments and exams leading to a knowledge that is cut-off from everyday reality.

Distant students need to become more selective and focused in their learning in order to master new information. The focus of their learning needs to shift them from a "surface approach" to a "deep approach". Morgan summarizes this approach as follows:

— Deep Approach:

— Focus on what is "signified" such as the instructor's arguments.

— Relate and distinguish new ideas and previous knowledge.

— Relate concepts to everyday experience.

— Relate and distinguish evidence and argument.

— Organize and structure content.

— Internal emphasis focusing on how instructional material relates to everyday reality.

The shift from "surface" to "deep" learning is not automatic. Brundage, Keane, and Mackneson suggest that adult students and their instructors must face and overcome a number of challenges before learning takes place including: becoming and staying responsible for themselves; "owning" their strengths, desires, skills, and needs; maintaining and increasing self-esteem; relating to others; clarifying what is learned; redefining what legitimate knowledge is; and dealing with content. These challenges are considered in relation to distance education:

— *Becoming and staying responsible for themselves.* High motivation is required to complete distant courses because the day-to-day contact with teachers and other students is typically lacking. Instructors can help motivate distant students by providing consistent and timely feedback, encouraging discussion among students, being well prepared for class, and by encouraging and reinforcing effective student study habits.

— *Owning one's strengths, desires, skills, needs.* Students need to recognize their strengths and limitations. They also need to understand their learning goals and objectives. The instructor can help distant students to explore their strengths/limitations and their learning goals/objectives by assuming a facilitative role in the learning process. Providing opportunities for students to share their personal learning goals and objectives for a course helps to make learning more meaningful and increases motivation.

— *Maintaining and increasing self-esteem.* Distant students may be afraid of their ability to do well in a course. They are balancing many responsibilities including employment and raising children. Often their involvement in distance education is unknown to those they work with and ignored by family members. Student performance is enhanced if learners set aside time for their instructional activities and if they receive family support in their academic endeavors. The instructor can maintain student self-esteem by providing timely feedback. It is critical for teachers to respond to students' questions, assignments, and concerns in a personalized and pleasant manner, using appropriate technology such as fax, phone, or computer. Informative comments that elaborate on the individual student's performance and suggest areas for improvement are especially helpful.

— *Relating to others.* Students often learn most effectively when they have the opportunity to interact with other students. Interaction among students typically leads to group problem solving. When students are unable to meet together, appropriate interactive technology such as E-mail should be provided to encourage small group and individual communication. Assignments in which students work together and then report back or present to the class as a whole, encourage student-to-student interaction. Ensure clear directions and realistic goals for group assignments.

— *Clarifying what is learned.* Distant students need to reflect on what they are learning. They need to examine the existing knowledge frameworks in their heads and how these are being added to or changed by incoming information. Examinations, papers, and class presentations provide opportunities for student and teacher to evaluate learning. However, less formal methods of evaluation will also help the students and teacher to understand learning. For example, periodically during the course the instructor can ask students to write a brief reflection on what they have learned and then provide an opportunity for them to share their insights with other class members.

— *Redefining what legitimate knowledge is.* Brundage, Keane, and Mackneson suggest that adult learners may find it difficult to accept that their own experience and reflections are legitimate knowledge. If the instructor takes a facilitative rather than authoritative role, students will see—their own experience as valuable and important to their further learning. Burge suggests having learners use first-person language to help them claim ownership of personal values, experiences, and insights.

— *Dealing with content.* Student learning is enhanced when content is related to examples. Instructors tend to teach using examples that were used when they received their training. For distance learning to be effective, however, instructors must discover examples that are relevant to their distant students. Encourage students to find or develop examples that are relevant to them or their community.

Because distance education is perceived as an increasingly effective method of instruction, educational researchers have examined the purposes and situations for which distance education is best suited. Research indicates that the instructional format itself has little effect on student achievement as long as the delivery technology is appropriate to the content being offered and all participants have access to the same technology.

Research suggests distant students bring basic characteristics to their learning experience which influence their success in coursework. Distance education students:

— Are voluntarily seeking further education.

— Have post-secondary education goals with expectations for higher grades.

— Are highly motivated and self-disciplined.

— Are older.

Studies also conclude that similar factors determine successful learning whether the students are distant or traditional. These factors include:

— Willingness to initiate calls to instructors for assistance.

— Possessing a more serious attitude toward the courses.

— Employment in a field where career advances can be readily "achieved through academic upgrading in a distance education environment".

— Previous completion of a college degree.

Good distance teaching practices are fundamentally identical to good traditional teaching practices and "those factors which influence good instruction may be generally universal across different environments and populations".Because distance education and its technologies require extensive planning and preparation, distance educators must consider the following in order to improve their effectiveness:

— Extensive pre-planning and formative evaluation is necessary. Teachers cannot "wing it". Distance learners value instructors who are well prepared and organized.

— Learners benefit significantly from a well-designed syllabus and presentation outlines. Structured note taking, using tools such as interactive study guides, and the use of visuals and graphics as part of the syllabus and presentation outlines contribute to student understanding of the course. However, these visuals must be tailored to the characteristics of the medium and to the characteristics of the students.

— Teachers must be properly trained both in the use of equipment and in those techniques proven effective in the distance education environment. Learners get more from the courses when the instructor seems comfortable with the technology, maintains eye contact with the camera, repeats questions, and possesses a sense of humor.

Many distant learners require support and guidance to make the most of their distance learning experiences. This support typically takes the form of some combination of student-instructor and student-student interaction. Research findings on the need for interaction have produced some important guidelines for instructors organizing courses for distant students:

— Learners value timely feedback regarding course assignments, exams, and projects.

— Learners benefit significantly from their involvement in small learning groups. These groups provide support and encouragement along with extra feedback on course assignments. Most importantly, the groups foster the feeling that if help is needed it is readily available.

- Learners are more motivated if they are in frequent contact with the instructor. More structured contact might be utilized as a motivational tool.
- Utilization of on-site facilitators who develop a personal rapport with students and who are familiar with equipment and other course materials increases student satisfaction with courses.
- The use of technologies such as fax machines, computers, and telephones can also provide learner support and interaction opportunities.

When establishing a distance education program, one of the first things considered is the cost of the system. Several cost components factor into the design of a distance education system:

- *Technology* - hardware (e.g., videotape players, cameras) and software (e.g., computer programs).
- *Transmission* - the on-going expense of leasing transmission access (e.g., T-1, satellite, microwave).
- *Maintenance* - repairing and updating equipment.
- *Infrastructure* - the foundational network and telecommunications infrastructure located at the originating and receiving campuses.
- *Production* - technological and personnel support required to develop and adapt teaching materials.
- *Support* - miscellaneous expenses needed to ensure the system works successfully including administrative costs, registration, advising/ counseling, local support costs, facilities, and overhead costs.

— *Personnel* - to staff all functions previously described.

Although the costs of offering distance education courses may be high, there are high costs associated with offering conventional courses.

Benefits of distance education courses to the learner include:

— Accessible training to students in rural areas.

— Students may complete their course of study without suffering the loss of salary due to relocation.

— Students are exposed to the expertise of the most qualified faculty.

Perhaps the question institutions must answer is whether it is part of their mission as educators to offer programs to those who might not be reached without distance education. The primary benefit to educational institutions through distance education may be the increased number of non-traditional students they are able to attract and serve.

The distance learning programs have sprung up and multiplied incredibly over the past ten years. However, despite its high profile in academe, distance learning remains highly controversial. Will it be the "savior" of the educational enterprise, or will it be the "destroyer" of the educational establishment as we know it? Will "virtual colleges and universities" replace brick and mortar, as some visionaries have asserted, or will it coexist with traditional educational systems?

The range of interpretations runs from sending an instructor some distance from the main campus to teach a group of students face-to-face to providing all instruction and interaction via the World Wide Web. Between these two extremes lie several different paradigms. First of all, sending faculty to teach at distant sites is no longer considered distance learning by most practitioners of the field. The current definition of the term usually includes physical separation of instructor and student and the use of some technological delivery system. Nonetheless, the patterns for instruction continue to expand based on local situations and funding. The most important factor, however, in whether a distance learning program grows or the direction it takes is most likely the administration and faculty of the college. Lacking sufficient support from either group will make the road rocky, if not impassible. At present colleges in the Tennessee Board of Regents System deliver distance learning courses basically four ways, but two modes dominate: Compressed video "smart classroom" transmissions over telephone lines and videotapes sent to the students' homes or placed in local libraries for use or checkout.

Most of the colleges are also trying to enter the on-line market as well, but the growth of on-line courses has been slow. Even with these systems, however, local modifications have been made to meet the needs of the colleges' students or to compromise for administration and faculty support. The first of these was broadcasting courses in the early morning and late evening via the local PBS station. Students came to campus for help sessions, test reviews and test taking, but the instruction was totally asynchronous. Next a lab-based independent telecourse program was developed which was very popular and became even more so when, in 1989, students were given the option to have the tapes checked out or mailed to them in their homes. A synchronous ITFS system which transmitted one-way video/two-way audio came on-line in 1985 and fed instruction to as many as seven different locations. Faculty liked this option because their role as 'the sage on the stage" continued, even if they could see only one section of their students. Until the video checkout system came into being, this was the most popular delivery system. However, once students could take courses "anytime, anyplace," the popularity of the ITFS system declined significantly.

In the early 1990s the college began experimenting with on-line course delivery. At first a 'bulletin board' system was set up, but it was 'clunky,' and students had many technical difficulties using it. Then the college contracted with an outside Internet service provider, and the system improved. Still, though, enrollments in the on-line classes have been small. The probable cause for this situation is hesitancy of faculty to try developing on-line courses, the desire of deans to keep as many students on campus as possible, and the fact that many students still do not have access to computers in the home Presently the college enrolls over 3000 students per year in distance learning, primarily through the videocourse option and a small number of on-line courses. The local cable company also donates airtime to broadcast telecourses, if the college wishes. The IFS system has now been decommissioned and leased to a wireless cable operator who has been delayed in implementing the local operation due to red tape. Despite the negatives, however, the distance learning program here has flourished, partly because of the breadth of course offerings (83 at present) and because it provides the flexibility many students need. Although the two modes are primarily asynchronous, several hybrid patterns have evolved, with both advantages and disadvantages to each. Most of the videocourses are totally asynchronous except for the requirement of proctored testing. However, the program has worked out a system that allows students to be tested in their locations, with the designation of an approved proctor at an educational institution or library there.

The program has even developed a complete Forestry certificate with laboratories that may be completed without coming to campus. On the other hand, the Biology Department developed two anatomy and physiology courses which allow students to receive the instruction at home but require them to attend an on-campus lab once each week. While this option is very attractive to students in this area, it shuts out students from far away who have seen information about the courses in distance learning guides and would like to take the courses. If other colleges begin to offer these courses totally asynchronously through interactive on-line labs or through partnering with other colleges for teaching the labs, will the faculty here decide to try a new approach or will the courses fail to grow because potential students from outside the local area have a better option?

Another similar hybrid delivery system has been very well received by area employers. This arrangement pairs videotapes and workbooks for home use with 'live' company-site laboratories using company equipment. Individuals taking these courses may opt for a certificate in six industrial maintenance fields or an Industrial Maintenance Technology Associate of Science degree. The popularity of this arrangement stems from the fact that workers do not have to leave the worksite to take the classes, and they receive both fundamental concepts as well as application of those concepts to machinery used at the company. Labs are provided by a 'traveling' instructor paired with an in-house 'expert' at the company location. Even within the on-line offerings at Chattanooga State several delivery patterns have emerged. One instructor holds class one night a week in a chat room on 'America On-Line.' He requires outside assignments that are shared during the "class" and brings in "guest speakers" on a frequent basis. Another instructor has placed everything on-line, including tests. Another uses a videocourse for instruction, with email interaction and submission of work. Another has developed a model which requires students to do research on the Web, read and analyze cases in a text, and participate asynchronously in a newsgroup once each week.

The distance learning program allows them to take more courses, complete degrees more quickly, or work around the circumstances in their lives. What does the future hold for distance learning in the new millennium? That will depend, on the continued mind-boggling pace of development of new technologies, such as WebTV, and the 'greening' of faculties around the country as 'old heads' retire and new, more technologically literate young instructors replace them. Finally, the issues of financing technology and instructional integrity will play pivotal roles in thwarting or expanding the role of distance learning for future students.

2

Web-oriented Distance Learning

The Internet is the world's largest, most powerful computer network connecting personal computers, sophisticated mainframes, and high speed supercomputers around the globe. The arrival of the World Wide Web signals the beginning of some fundamental changes in how teaching, training, and self-directed learning will occur at all ages and stages of life. The World Wide Web as a vehicle for disseminating course materials and for creating active learning experiences within a classroom-based course.

Educators at all levels, from Kindergarten to adult training, are drawing a distinction between two fundamentally different approaches to teaching. In one, the goal is to transfer, as effectively and efficiently as possible, a concise and coherent block of information from the teacher or computer into the minds of the learners. Most existing computer-based training for adults has been designed with knowledge transfer in mind. Extraneous information is left out.

The emphasis is on individual learning and learners have a limited number of paths through the lesson. This approach works well for the training of basic skills in areas of knowledge that are well defined and stable. For most of us, though, the world just isn't that way. As adults we face one ill-defined problem after another. The specific facts that we have to know change so quickly that some knowledge becomes obsolete almost as soon as we master it. The knowledge-transfer approach doesn't prepare us well for a messy world in constant motion.

Constructivism

An alternative way to think about teaching and learning is called constructivism. A constructivist trainer doesn't strip away the natural complexity of a subject. Instead, multiple perspectives are brought to bear. The goal of a constructivist learning environment is not the accurate transfer of content from the instructor to the learner. Instead, the learner is given tasks and opportunities, information resources and support, and is encouraged to construct their own version of the content, subject to revision through feedback. Many paths through the lesson are allowed and collaboration with other learners is stressed over lonely individual learning.

A constructivist use of technology presents information to the learner in multiple forms from multiple sources and invites the learner to make sense of it. The learner can acquire the information needed from several sources via the computer, and from off-line sources including his or her own prior experience, from information gathered while collaborating with other learners, and from references and other sources of expertise found somewhere far away from the computer screen.

In general, a constructivist approach is more learner-focused, and less teacher-focused. The emphasis is on making a set of tasks and resources available to learners, and creating an environment in which the learners can actively create their own meaning in that context, rather than to passively absorb knowledge structures created by the instructor. In this approach, the instructor's role moves toward being a coach and orchestrator of resources, and moves away from being the sole source of information. The emphasis is on cases studies, problem solving, and the creation of meaning.

In the last two years, a new technology has grown enormously in importance and accessibility. This technology, the World Wide Web, lends itself beautifully to constructivist, active learning. The World Wide Web is a part - the fastest growing part - of the internet.

In 1989, a group of scientists at the European Laboratory for Particle Physics (CERN) in Geneva, Switzerland began developing an Internet tool that would link information produced by all of the CERN researchers. The tool provided a way to link textual information on different computers and created by different scientists. The object was to overcome issues of incompatibility and utilize a new way of linking made possible by computers, called "hypertext". Rather than presenting information in a linear or hierarchical fashion, hypertext permits information to be linked in a web-like structure.

Nodes of information can be linked to other nodes of information in multiple ways. As a result, users can dynamically criss-cross the information web using pieces in the order most convenient to them. The CERN project resulted in an innovative front-end to the Internet, now referred to as the World-Wide Web (WWW). The WWW provides users with a uniform and convenient means of accessing the vast resources of the Internet.

In 1993, the National Center for Supercomputing Applications (NCSA) at the University of Illinois pushed the CERN scientists' idea further by creating a software tool called Mosaic. Mosaic is an easy to use graphical user interface that permits text, graphics, sound and video to be hyperlinked. Mosaic was the first of the Internet tools that are now referred to as " Web browsers". Other well-known browsers include Netscape (the first commercial browser developed by some of the programmers involved with the Mosaic project) and Microsoft's Internet Explorer.

Web browsers permit users to connect to the Internet and facilitate accessing information located on another remote computer. The Web browser links to the remote computer just long enough so that the information you need can be sent to your computer for you to view. Documents created to be viewed by a browser are formatted using Hypertext Markup Language (HTML).

HTML solves incompatibility problems by using standardized tags which indicate such things as whether a piece of text should be plain, bold, italic, or linked to another piece of text. Pages of information on a computer formatted with HTML and accessible to someone with a Web browser, are referred to as "home pages" or "Web pages".

The WWW and Web browsers have made the Internet a more user-friendly environment. The ability to integrate graphics, text, and sound into a single tool means that novice users do not have to struggle with such a steep learning curve. In addition, organizations and individuals can create home pages independently and link to other home pages on their own computers or to pages created by others on different computer systems.

For educators, the WWW provides an exciting new opportunity for distance teaching and learning. The WWW can be used by the distance educator to build a classroom home page. The home page can cover information about the class including the syllabus, exercises, literature references, and instructor's biography. The instructor can also provide links to information on the WWW that would be useful to students in the class (e.g., research data on agricultural markets, global climate change, or space missions). Other links can access library catalogs or each student's individual home page. In addition, the home page can link students to a discussion list or listserv that set up for student communication. It is also a relatively simple matter to use the homepage to create forms that students can fill out and that will end up being sent to you as an e-mail message.

A web server can be run on a personal computer or a UNIX workstation. The server need not be a fast, expensive machine. In fact, I set up my first server on a six year old Macintosh SE/30. When the traffic grew to the point of justifying the investment, we upgraded to a faster machine. Setting up a server is a fairly simple task, and corporations, university departments, and even elementary schools are doing it every day.

What makes the World Wide Web especially exciting is that it also allows you to create anchors that download files for you or allow you to send e-mail to an individual. The web thus makes it easy to gain access to data, software and people. It's a user-friendly front end to almost everything on the internet. Within a year or so, the mechanics of creating documents on the web will become transparent.

Most publishers of word processing software are adding the capability of saving documents in web format to their ever-growing list of features. So far, however, the end result of using a word processor to create web pages directly may not be exactly what you had in mind. An active webwriter will want to know how to tweak the appearance of the documents and, for the moment, that requires some familiarity with HTML. HTML, or HyperText Markup Language, is easy to learn.

To prepare a page for the web, you just embed special characters or tags in your document to tell your browser how to display a given word. For a computer trainer, learning the basics of HTML should take no longer than a weekend. Excellent resources for learning HTML can be found on the web, and are indexed in A Primer for Creating Web Resources. The Web 66 Internet Server Cookbook contains recipes for putting pictures and sounds in your pages, serving downloadable files, and maintaining a server from a distance.

An alternative method for displaying content on the web is the Adobe Acrobat format. This allows complex page layouts to be used, but users of your materials must all have the proper helper application installed on their machines. In a corporate environment with software standards in place, this shouldn't be a problem. Once you have created your pages, you simply upload them to the server you'll be using.

Most medium to large-sized corporations have already established a web presence, and many smaller companies have as well. Whether you purchase space on the machines of an internet provider or set up your own webserver, you need not be physically near the server itself. Most maintenance can be done from a distance. Once the use of the web as a way to distribute course materials is second nature to you, the next phase is to take advantage of all the material that's out there beyond the walls of your institution.

The more you incorporate such activities into your course, the more it will become transformed into an learner-centered environment and the less often you'll find yourself holding forth on center stage. If you can get friends and colleagues, both in and outside of your enterprise, to volunteer to answer questions, you've broadened the pool of experience available to your students.

Newsgroups provide an invisible college of people helping people. They are a great source of up to the minute news about software releases, bugs, and workarounds. If you have your own newsserver, you can also set up internal newsgroups specific to your course to provide a space for students to exchange information on an ongoing basis. Most newsgroups maintain a list of frequently asked questions that have come up within that group. These can be a rich source of materials and pointers to other resources on the web. Most major software publishers (e.g., Microsoft, Novell, Claris, Adobe) have placed their technical notes on the web.

Patches, applications, utilities, documentation... there are many sources of useful wares ready to be downloaded. FTPing (i.e., grabbing) and decompressing this software is handled transparently by your web browser. You can place an anchor on a page that refers to a file and all your users have to do is click on it to have it delivered to their desktop. Suppose you're teaching a course on desktop publishing and you want your students to have the experience of dealing with a difficult client. One way to bring that kind of encounter into the classroom is to set up an e-mail address with a fabricated name. Periodically, you answer the mail at that account while acting like someone else.

Distance educators who are ready to develop a web presence, should avoid the following pitfalls:

- *Rushing in without a master plan*: Don't get so caught up in learning HTML and developing the home page that the purpose for developing your presence on the WWW is lost. Spend less time struggling with HTML, developing amusing graphics or playing with possible background and more time considering the purpose and content of the home page.
- *Before you start your home page*: Think about your reason for developing a Web presence. Sound instructional design principles apply to home pages just as with any other materials prepared for a course. Become familiar with new software tools for developing home pages. Computer software tools such as HotMetal and HotDog mean that anyone familiar with using word processing software can develop a good looking and functional home page.

Utilize information that already has been developed for your course. If you already have your notes and syllabi in word processed form, make use of tools such as HotDog to format them for distribution on the WWW.

Hundreds of home pages have already been developed for courses. Some of these home pages allow students to complete an entire course from the WWW and others are developed in conjunction with lectures delivered on-campus or by video or audio.

Utilizing a consistent format for each of your pages. Based on suggestions made by the above mentioned style manuals, develop a consistent format for each web page. While colored or patterned backgrounds can be used on homepages, plain grey or white backgrounds make text easier to read. Keeping page lengths short. Your main index should jump to a lot of shorter pages. In cases where page information is long, index internally so that the student can jump to specific information as needed. Maximizing links to internal information and minimizing links to external information. The purpose of your home page is to provide information on a specific subject area. Only provide external links to home pages that provide useful related information for your students.

The home page should help your students to find necessary course information, learn the material, and get involved in thinking about the course material. Properly designed home pages will encourage thought, discussion and active participation by your distant students. The following elements can be included in your class home page:

— *Course & Instructor Information* — Include such items as course topics to be covered, your office hours, textbook information, course objectives, and grading policies.

— *Class Communication* — Provide access to your e-mail, link to discussion groups that you have set up for student-to-student communication, and create forms that your students can use to report problems or provide biographical information about themselves.

— *Assignments and Tests* — Distribute assignments and tests, provide for online completion or submission, and give solutions, hints, or samples of what you expect.

— *Material covered in the classroom* — Make lecture notes and handouts available either as web pages or as downloadable files.

— *Demonstrations, Animation, Video, Audio* — This is more complex than other suggestions and will require that your students have access to computers with sound and video cards.

— *Reference Material* — List materials in print and electronic form that supplement the textbook. To avoid copyright problems, electronic articles should either be written by you or in the public domain (e.g., government documents or are already available on the WWW with author's permission to distribute). In addition, provide links to other pages which cover information on the topic, similar courses that may also be available on WWW, your university library, and other on-campus resources that may help your student complete the course.

For many people who are new to the web, the temptation to browse and pursue one link after another is so strong that they spend countless hours glued to the screen. In an educational or training situation, however, we don't have the luxury of spending all of our time that way. As much as we value curiosity and exploration, it's necessary for us to find ways to get the greatest learning benefit from the web in the shortest possible time. At San Diego State University we've been thinking about how to do that, and one lesson format that we've developed toward that goal is called a WebQuest. A WebQuest is an activity of guided inquiry in which learners are given a task which requires internet access to complete.

WebQuests can be designed as short- or long-term activities. At the end of a short term WebQuest, a learner will have grappled with a significant amount of new information and made sense of it. A short-term WebQuest is designed to be completed in one to three class periods. WebQuests are deliberately designed to make the best use of a learner's time. There is questionable educational benefit in having learners surf the net without a clear task in mind, and most educational and training institutions must ration student connect time severely. To achieve that efficiency and clarity of purpose, WebQuests should contain at least the following parts:

— An introduction that sets the stage and provides some background information.

— A task that is doable and interesting. The task could include a series of questions that must be answered, a summary to be created, a problem to be solved, a position to be formulated and defended, a creative work, or anything that requires the learners to process and transform the information they've gathered.

— A set of information resources needed to complete the task. Many (though not necessarily all) of the resources are embedded in the WebQuest document itself as anchors pointing to information on the World Wide Web. Information sources might include web documents, experts available via e-mail or realtime conferencing, searchable databases on the net, and books and other documents physically available in the learner's setting.

— A description of the process to follow to complete the WebQuest.

— Some learning advice on how to organize the information acquired. This can take the form of guiding questions, or directions to complete organizational frameworks such as timelines, concept maps, or cause-and-effect diagrams.

— A conclusion that summarizes what they will have accomplished or learned by completing this WebQuest.

It is a simple matter to place a form on the web that collects information from your learners. To actually send that information to the server and process it, though, goes beyond simple HTML into the realm of CGI: the Common Gateway Interface.

It is here that most web developers stop because creating CGI programs at this point requires the ability to program in C, Perl, or AppleScript. As time goes on there will be ready-made CGI's available to accomplish most tasks, but for the near term there's a learning curve here that stops most people.

Future of Net-Based Training

The net world is moving quickly towards greater interactivity and sensory engagement. There are several developments worth watching.

Some websites allow you to click on a picture and hear a greeting or introduction in the form of a sound file. You have to wait for the file to download before hearing anything, though, which tries the patience of all but the most fervent websurfers.

RealAudio is different. It begins to stream audio to your workstation almost immediately. It's like radio on demand. For distance education, the usefulness of RealAudio is obvious. All of the spoken communication that makes up a bulk of a traditional class can be digitized and made available as needed. As long as this doesn't lead back to the "talk, chalk and a hairy arm" tradition, RealAudio could become a standard feature of distance education on the web.

Virtual Reality Modelling Language is an embryonic set of tools and conventions for portraying three-dimensional space on the web. Instead of seeing a static picture, you'll be able to hold your mouse down over a graphic and see it from multiple perspectives, zooming in for detail and veering in any direction.

For distance education, this allows for a more intuitive depiction of content: imagine seeing bubbles labeled with all the major concepts in your course. Lines linking the bubbles represent the relationships among them. Zoom in on a bubble and you've arrived at a webpage describing it in more detail. You might also use VRML to create a simulated learning environment with a reference room, laboratory, and help desk.

Java is a language for writing small programs (applets) that are downloaded as part of a web page. This will allow the web to take on most of the characteristics of the interactive multimedia you would find on a CD-ROM.

MOO stands for Multi-user dimension, Object-Oriented, which doesn't at first convey much about its meaning. A MOO is a shared virtual space that people can help create from their own computers. You can set up your conference room the way you like it and invite others to join you there. At present, most MOOs are text-based. When they begin to become more graphical, (soon) they will become the most popular places to be in cyberspace. These developments, and others, will make distance education more and more practicable on the web as time goes on.

Building the Information Driveway

New technologies with new applications can significantly reduce the costs of school networking and significantly improve the networking capabilities available to students, teachers, and the general public. These economies will make it possible to provide universal access to educational networks, thereby advancing the causes of educational equity and school reform and ending the isolation of the traditional classroom.

During the last few years, thousands of schools and hundreds of thousands of students and teachers have begun to develop the Internet into a major educational resource. Within the community of educational researchers, the Internet is now an accepted standard. Network use is also growing rapidly throughout the larger educational community, but several factors have placed practical limits on this growth. This paper attempts to identify some of these limiting factors and suggest new technologies that can help schools surmount these obstacles.

Consider first some of the reasons that propel educational use of the Internet. These include the following:

— *Isolation*: Wide-area computer networks can help end the isolation of students and teachers in the traditional classroom. Of course, networks will accomplish this end only if they are inexpensive enough to be made available to all students and teachers.

— *Equity*: Connecting all schools to the Internet will provide equity of access to online information and create opportunities for all schools to publish online. This requires a reasonably priced infrastructure that all schools can afford to purchase, install, and maintain.

— *Reform:* Networks can be a powerful tool in support of educational reform. A widespread network infrastructure with easy access to information servers and tools for placing resources on servers will allow students, classes, and teachers to produce online materials, do extensive collaborative work, and broadly share instructional resources.

Schools face possible obstacles in each of these areas. If a school cannot obtain adequate connectivity, its ability to overcome isolation will be limited. If it has no access to a server, its ability to publish materials online will be limited. If it has too few user devices for all students to participate in networking activities, the promise of equity will not be achieved. And if tools do not exist that enable students and teachers to use networks imaginatively and effectively to support their broader educational goals, the promise of educational reform will not be met.

Overcoming each of these obstacles entails a technological challenge. In the following sections, we list these challenges and describe some mechanisms for meeting them. Underlying arguments is a common theme of shared infrastructure and shared support mechanisms.

Networking is a means of building community, and a strong sense of community is often the key to building viable network-linked educational programs and resources and sustaining them over the long term. The types of educational and community networks that we advocate differ in some essential ways from those developed for many commercial applications. Commercial networks emphasize privacy and security issues over cost and access considerations. For educational and community networks, cost and access are the primary concerns, and network architectures that neglect these factors are unlikely to be sustainable for very long. Shared infrastructure and broad applicability bring other educational benefits. They create network environments that are conducive to interdisciplinary and collaborative activities and to research projects that explore an ever-expanding scope of resources. We believe that these sorts of activities and projects can contribute effectively to educational reform. We find that the portions of networks with the highest development costs and the greatest need for cost reduction are precisely those with the fewest possibilities for shared infrastructure. To put the issue in colloquial terms, we must deal not so much with the problem of building the information superhighway as with building the information driveway that leads into the home or classroom. Once this part of network connectivity is established, there remains the task of using it effectively to access online material and produce materials for others to use.

Two factors dramatically affect the performance and affordability of internetworking: the cost and bandwidth of the 'local loop' from the user's site to the nearest network point of presence, and the existence of a complementary wide-area infrastructure to tie the various local loops together. These two factors are critical regardless of the specific details of the chosen technology or the market position of the service provider. Schools and communities should choose their network technologies and services strategically, with an eye toward how their choices will support and leverage the overall networking infrastructure. Broad infrastructure needs are a much more important consideration in developing educational and community networks than in planning private networks or networks that serve a limited number of public or nonprofit organisations. Even though educational programs have a specific focus, they inspire other activities, and they rely on other organisations for many kinds of resources. Hence, it is important to consider the entire community as a unit when assessing alternatives for providing an economical infrastructure for school or community networking.

— *We take up the issue of providing the local loop:* Several factors make it likely that the costs of providing connectivity will drop, perhaps dramatically, in the next few years. One strong influence is market competition to supply the local loop. Where there are multiple suppliers of connectivity to schools, homes, or offices, competitive forces will help reduce the cost of network services to these sites. Many communities are experiencing active competition in this area, although recent federal telecommunications legislation may allow the reestablishment of monopolies of local connectivity,

> with a corresponding decrease in options and likely increase in price. One must also take care to distinguish competition in the local loop from competition in limited market segments, such as voice or video services. While this latter form of competition could decrease the price of specific services, it may have no relevance to data services and internetworking. More typically, some service providers may engage in 'cream-skimming'—seeking to exploit market segments with the highest profit margins, a practice which public utility commissions and local regulatory authorities should probably discourage.

Tariff policies also affect the viability of various options for Internet access. For example, the commonly available digital telephone service known as ISDN can provide economical connectivity at moderate bandwidths, as long as its tariffs are set at an affordable flat rate (with no time charges). When time charges are applied, this service becomes uneconomical for typical network interconnects, since it is desirable to keep the connection in place throughout the day.

Competition to provide local loops is likely to involve a number of new technologies. Telephone subscribers can employ new electronics—most notably, a technology known in telephonic circles as High-bit-rate Digital Subscriber Loop (HDSL)—to wring vastly higher data rates out of older copper infrastructure. HDSL can provide data services at speeds in excess of one megabit per second and costs as low as one-tenth those of traditional connections. Public utility commissions will ultimately determine whether these economies result in savings for home, school, and office subscribers or in larger profits for telephone companies. This is a complex issue, since rates are determined not only by the intrinsic cost of any single service to the telephone company, but also by the fraction of equipment and maintenance left in the hands of the customer, the need to subsidize certain lifeline services, and the need to average rates across the many different technologies used to supply local loops for a given region. In addition to HDSL, which provides a symmetrical service, there are also asymmetrical services, such as Asymmetric Digital Subscriber Loop (ADSL). Symmetrical services provide the same data rate into and out of a given site.

Asymmetrical services typically provide higher data rates into a given site than out of it. While asymmetrical services may be acceptable for a residence, where the users are mostly consumers of information, they would not be appropriate for connections to local area networks at schools and libraries because they would limit the ability to publish information at these sites. And although some ADSL technologies have much higher bandwidths than HDSL, they provide significantly higher speeds only in the forward (outward) direction, and they cannot drive data for the distances that HDSL can. A new service known as SDSL promises to offer the bandwidth advantages of ADSL in a symmetrical mode. Another promising development in the field of telephony is the deployment of fiber optics, either to drop points in the neighborhood or to the curbside of subscriber homes or offices. Fiber brings vastly higher bandwidth than copper and promises higher reliability over time.

Once the capital costs of laying this new infrastructure are depreciated, suppliers can anticipate significant reductions in the costs of providing high bandwidth data services, namely those with speeds in excess of one million bits per second. Such services would exhaust only a tiny fraction of the bandwidth available through a fiber infrastructure, which can also provide video services requiring the equivalent of tens of millions of bits per second. Some telephone companies are contemplating a fiber optic/coaxial cable hybrid system, an architecture commonly used by newer cable television installations. These systems provide a particularly attractive architecture for data services and internetworking: they can offer services with peak bandwidths of 10 to 40 million bits per second or higher, at prices potentially competitive with those of present-day analog telephone service. Widespread deployment of such systems will help redefine the pricing structure for high-bandwidth data services, as prices drop as low as a few percent of current service offerings.

With extensive deployment, the cable modems needed to deliver this service can be marketed at prices comparable to those of conventional modems, and the service itself can be sold for prices comparable to those of premium cable channels. Where internal wiring is costly to install and where external connectivity is difficult to achieve through fixed links, wireless technologies offer an attractive option. With its ease of setup, wireless is particularly appealing in situations where costly and time-consuming building modifications are necessary to install internal wiring. Wireless links can also be used to provide pieces of a metropolitan area network infrastructure. But one must bear in mind that maintenance costs for wireless links are likely to be higher than those for fixed wiring and that the bandwidth available for wireless communications is extremely limited compared to the bandwidth of fixed copper or fiber infrastructure. This important point has been largely overlooked by groups advocating wireless technologies as a panacea for public network access. These technologies offer an excellent starting point for such access, but as usage grows, the bandwidth available through this medium will inevitably become saturated, and the majority of public Internet traffic will have to be transferred to traditional fixed communications links. Thus, there will have to be truly compelling reasons to deploy wireless communications between fixed points in a metropolitan area.

Wireless technologies can be used effectively, however, as a rapid enabler, a temporary connection that can serve a networking purpose while fixed wiring is being planned and installed. Upon completion of wiring, the wireless apparatus might be reused to help leverage another start-up site. New technologies are also generating new means of tying together local loops to form a wide-area networking infrastructure. New telephone architectures offer the possibility of significantly reduced costs for data services and internetworking. The traditional telephone infrastructure connects lines from homes and offices to switches at the telephone company's central offices, forming circuits through which telephone calls are routed. This circuit-switched infrastructure is oriented toward point-to-point connections, with endpoints that may be very widely separated. Each connection ties up switch and transmission resources for the duration of the connection, regardless of how much information is being passed through the circuit. Internet services are based upon a quite different architecture, one that involves a common 'cloud' of connectivity through which individual data packets are routed to their final destinations. This packet-switched infrastructure offers a number of significant advantages for data transmission.

Individual circuits need not be maintained, so there are lower costs in terms of switches and infrastructure relating to the transmission plant. Demands are made upon this infrastructure only during the actual transmission of data packets. Furthermore, thanks to the manner in which Internet protocols behave in the presence of traffic congestion, the system can be overloaded briefly with only a slowdown in the rate of data transmission as opposed to a failure to establish a desired connection. This type of packet-switched infrastructure can be provided through a number of technologies commonly offered by the telephone industry and referred to collectively as 'fast packet services.' The optimal mix of technologies will depend upon local pricing and needs. More important than specific programmatic needs may be the overall strategies employed to provide connectivity to schools and community centers in a given area. The following points are relevant for schools and communities developing strategies for connectivity:

— *Local points of presence:* Nearby access to the internet cloud lowers the cost of the local loop by reducing the need for long distance or local measured calls. Ideally, any telephone company çentral office should provide an entry point to the internet. This is likely to be a very cost-effective mechanism for the commodity provision of Internet access.

— *Shared infrastructure:* Possibilities for shared infrastructure include shared bandwidth for links among central offices, shared modem pools for dial-up connectivity, and shared points of public access.

— *Local aggregation of traffic:* School districts can aggregate traffic and purchase bulk connectivity to pass this traffic to the Internet cloud. Municipal governments can play a similar role for community centers and government offices. These groups assume a portion of the responsibility for network management and thereby reduce costs for the end users.

By working with local telephone suppliers and following these guidelines, communities can provide good connectivity at modest cost.

Connectivity alone does not create a networked environment of value to schools and communities. More important is the quality of information available over the network and the ability of schools and communities to use the network as their own publishing venue. The content challenge involves a set of technical issues, which we discuss in this section, and a number of social issues, which lie beyond the scope of this paper. These social issues relate to the evolution of the network community, the formation of networked collaborations, and the financing of network resources that exploit the full richness and depth of the medium.

Technological factors can assist in these areas, but human factors ultimately will determine the network's success and relevance. The architecture of low-cost online services is increasingly dominated by client/server mechanisms for delivering information. Determining the costs of such services requires an analysis of the costs of the client and server machines and the availability of software suitable to provide these services. We consider first the question of client machines or access devices. Computers can be bought now for $1,000 to $2,000. This has been true for the last half-dozen years, and it is likely to remain true as long as the only forces governing these prices are traditional computer marketplace forces. It is not the price of the raw materials or the manufacturing cost that determines the retail price of personal computers. Rather, marketing strategies and advertising decisions set these prices. Producing a $200 user device capable of running a World Wide Web browser over standard telephone links is within the realm of possibility, provided that a large enough market exists for such a device.

Many forces are converging to make it likely that such devices will be produced. These include the progress of game machines, which now typically contain powerful graphics computers as a standard component, the development of set-top boxes for cable television systems, and the need of schools for large numbers of cheap, networked computers. With the rapid evolution of computer hardware, operating systems, and software, it is possible to pass still-serviceable hardware from business and government offices into the hands of schools and community groups, who could use it to gain basic Internet access at extremely low cost. The advent of Windows 95, with its significant new hardware demands, is beginning to drive many commercial users to invest in new hardware. But much of the remaindered hardware is still capable of running the older Windows operating system and supporting graphical interfaces to Internet resources. If commercial users donated remaindered hardware to schools and community centers, and if mechanisms to support this hardware were put in place, it might be possible to rapidly provide network access to all of the nation's classrooms.

There are many uncertainties associated with such a scheme. It assumes that the evolution of software for classroom application will be much slower than the evolution of commercial software, so that the Windows machines will be adequate for most educational applications for a number of years. And it assumes that new features in commercial software will not make the training that students receive with older machines and software irrelevant to the commercial workplace.

Finally, it assumes that older machines can be supplied in quantities sufficient to provide school districts with a uniform and supportable computing environment. If these conditions can be met, the donation of older equipment could provide a significant boost to school and community networking efforts. This is only an interim approach and a partial solution for school and community networking, but it should allow communities to stretch significantly the dollars available for networking projects. Whether the client machines are standard office computers or low-cost school and home computers, they will require affordable client software in order to access common information services. Under one widely used marketing model that works to the advantage of educational users, software vendors charge a fee for their server software but give away client software free of charge to all users or, more commonly, to educational users.

The rationale for this pricing model is that it encourages access to online information, for which there may be an access fee. Vendors may also charge a fee for the construction of servers to groups that place information online for commercial access. Under this type of pricing arrangement, it is possible for educational users to obtain high quality World Wide Web and Geographical Information System browsers, among others. The practical consequence is that the client code is free to educational users but is well-maintained to insure the availability of solid code for all commercial clients. Whether the market will continue to support this type of pricing structure depends largely on whether the majority of vendors adhere to standards for transporting information over the network. If large volumes of material are available through a small set of common standard protocols, there are likely to be low-cost or free products available to implement these standards. If one vendor obtains a near monopoly on the market, there is a danger of that vendor introducing proprietary protocols in its products and forcing educational users to purchase them at arbitrarily high prices. We would regard this as a classic monopoly situation that could be addressed under existing antitrust laws.

On the server side, there is a relatively broad range of options, consistent with the idea that one need support only a small set of network protocols to supply a very wide range of information services. With an increasing number of vendors supplying Internet servers for school use, we are fast approaching the possibility of a generic Internet server. Generic servers can be built on the most common hardware platforms with public domain operating systems at a fraction of the cost of servers commonly available just a year or two ago. Current networking projects and forthcoming network products are likely to produce enough examples of server setup and maintenance to make their operation practical in any school or school district. Further simplification of this task will occur as new software is developed to facilitate the management of these machines, both locally at the school site and remotely from a district office or contracted system management provider. Some vendors provide free client software but extract a fee, sometimes a very large one, for the server software. Fortunately, many vendors are adjusting server charges based on the features offered and the audience likely to use them. For example, systems that include advanced security features for financial transactions are likely to be sold at higher prices than systems meant for simpler information delivery systems. Here, too, adherence to a small set of network protocols makes it likely that low-cost or free implementation of information services will be available to educational and community networks. It is important to realise that services like the World Wide Web have their limitations, too, and to consider mechanisms that will help overcome these limitations for educational and community users. Advances are also being made in the area of Web editors, which simplify the task of creating resources to be placed online via the World Wide Web. These advances are reducing the costs of training students and teachers to create multimedia presentations for online distribution and increasing their ability to develop these resources as part of their standard classroom activities. A number of vendors have announced products in this area.

Two important tasks must be accomplished in order to extend internet access to all students and teachers and enable them to incorporate internet resources and techniques into their everyday educational activities. Schools and homes must be provided with connectivity, and second, facilities must be developed that make it easy and inexpensive to create and access online resources. We believe that technologies exist to meet these goals—indeed, we believe that the ideals of universal connectivity for all the nation's classrooms and commonplace classroom use of the Internet can be realized by the end of the decade.

3

Development of Distance Learning

A distance educator can employ a number of strategies focusing on planning, student understanding, interaction, and teaching to ensure a successfully delivered course. Classroom teachers rely on a number of visual and unobtrusive cues from their students to enhance their delivery of instructional content. A quick glance, for example, reveals who is attentively taking notes, pondering a difficult concept, or preparing to make a comment. The student who is frustrated, confused, tired, or bored is equally evident. The attentive teacher consciously and subconsciously receives and analyzes these visual cues and adjusts the course delivery to meet the needs of the class during any particular lesson. In contrast, the distant teacher has few, if any, visual cues. Those cues that do exist are filtered through technological devices such as video monitors. It is difficult to carry on a stimulating teacher-class discussion when spontaneity is altered by technical requirements and distance. Without the use of a real-time visual medium such as television, the teacher receives no visual information from the distant sites. The teacher might never really know, for example, if students are asleep, talking among themselves, or even in the room. Separation by distance also affects the general rapport of the class. Living in different communities, geographic regions, or even states deprives the teacher and students of a common community link.

The challenges posed by distance teaching are countered by opportunities to reach a wider student audience; to meet the needs of students who are unable to attend on-campus classes; to involve outside speakers who would otherwise be unavailable; and to link students from different social, cultural, economic, and experiential backgrounds.

Many teachers feel the opportunities offered by distance education outweigh the obstacles. In fact, instructors often comment that the focused preparation required by distance teaching improves their overall teaching ability and empathy for their students. Instructional development is essential in distance education, where the instructor and students may share limited common background and typically have minimal face-to-face contact. Although instructional development models and processes abound, the majority follow the same basic stages of design, development, evaluation, and revision.

The Design Stage

— *Determine the need for instruction* - To begin, determine the need for instruction by considering what external data verify the need, what factors led to the instructional need, and what past experiences indicate that the instruction being planned can effectively meet this need.

— *Analyze your audience* - To better understand the distant learners and their needs, consider their ages, cultural backgrounds, past experiences, interests and educational levels. Assess their familiarity with the various instructional methods and delivery systems being considered, determine how they will apply the knowledge gained in the course, and note whether the class will consist of a broad mix of students or discrete subgroups with different characteristics (e.g. urban/rural, undergraduate/graduate). When possible, the instructor should visit distant sites and interview prospective students, both individually and in small groups. This personalized attention will also show students that the instructor is more than an anonymous presence, linked by electronic technology. Colleagues who have worked with the target population can also offer advice.

— *Establish instructional goals/objectives* - Based on the nature of the problem as well as student needs and characteristics, establish instructional goals and objectives. Goals are broad statements of instructional intent, while objectives are specific steps leading to goal attainment.

The Development Stage

— *Create a content outline* - Based on the instructional problems, the audience analysis, instructional goals and objectives, and an understanding of the desired course content, create an outline of the content to be covered.

— *Review existing materials* - Next, the instructor should review existing materials. Instructional materials should not be used solely because they are readily available or have been effective in a traditional classroom setting. This is especially true if pre-packaged materials, such as telecourses, are being considered. Whereas many pre-packaged instructional tools are developed and marketed to reach students with similar backgrounds and experiences, they may have little relevance for distant learners who come to the course with widely varied and non-traditional experiential backgrounds. If pre-packaged materials are to be used, consider developing "wrap around" introductions, conclusions, and summaries that specifically relate the learning materials to the instructional context of the distant student.

— *Organize and develop content* - Perhaps the greatest challenge facing the distance educator is creating student-relevant examples. Content, for the most part, is taught using examples that relate the content to a context understood by the students. The best examples are "transparent", allowing the learners to focus on the content being presented. If examples are irrelevant, learning is impeded. This is a special challenge in rural and multicultural settings where the teacher's realm of experience and related content examples may be foreign to distant learners. To address this problem, discuss potential content examples with a sampling of the target audience.

— *Select/develop materials and methods* - The development of instructional materials and selection of delivery methods will often require integrating print, voice, video, and data technology in concert with face-to-face communication. The challenge here is to integrate delivery components, based on identifiable learner needs, content requirements, and technical constraints. For example, it does little good to rely on delivery technology that is unavailable to some class members. Make sure the same delivery systems are available to all distant learners to avoid the need to create parallel learning experiences.

The Evaluation Stage

— *Review goals and objectives* - One purpose of evaluation is to determine if the instructional methods and materials are accomplishing the established goals and objectives. Implementation of instruction represents the first real test of what has been developed. Try to pre-test instruction on a small scale prior to implementation. If this is not possible, the first actual use will also serve as the "field test" for determining effectiveness.

— *Develop an evaluation strategy* - Plan how and when to evaluate the effectiveness of the instruction. Formative evaluation can be used to revise instruction as the course is being developed and implemented. For example, the distance educator can give students pre-addressed and stamped postcards to complete and mail after each session. These "mini-evaluations" might focus on course strengths and weaknesses, technical or delivery concerns, and content areas in need of further coverage. Summative evaluation is conducted after instruction is completed and provides a data base for course revision and future planning. Following course completion, consider a summative evaluation session in which students informally brainstorm ways to improve the course. Consider having a local facilitator run the evaluation session to encourage a more open discussion.

Within the context of formative and summative evaluation, data are collected through quantitative and qualitative methods. Quantitative evaluation relies on a breadth of response and is patterned after experimental research focused on the collection and manipulation of statistically relevant quantities of data. In contrast, qualitative evaluation focuses on a depth of response, using more subjective methods such as interviews and observation to query a smaller number of respondents in greater depth.

Qualitative approaches may be of special value because the diversity of distant learners may defy relevant statistical stratification and analysis. The best approach often combines quantitative measurement of student performance with open-ended interviewing and non-participant observation to collect and assess information about attitudes toward the course's effectiveness and the delivery technology.

— *Collect and analyze evaluation data* - Following implementation of your course/materials, collect the evaluation data. Careful analysis of these results will identify gaps or weaknesses in the instructional process. It is equally important to identify strengths and successes. Results of the evaluation analysis will provide a "springboard" from which to develop the revision plan.

The Revision Stage

There is room for improvement in even the most carefully developed distance delivered course, and the need for revision should be anticipated. In fact, there will likely be more confidence in a course that has been significantly revised than in one considered flawless the first time through.

Revision plans typically are a direct result of the evaluation process in tandem with feedback from colleagues and content specialists. The best source of revision ideas may be the instructor's own reflection on course strengths and weaknesses. For this reason, revision should be planned as soon as possible after course completion.

Often, course revisions will be minor, such as breaking a large and unwieldy instructional unit into more manageable components, increasing assignment feedback, or improving student-to-student interaction. On other occasions, major revisions will be needed. Significant course changes should be field-tested prior to future course use.

Test revision ideas on small groups of distant learners, content specialists, and colleagues. Results of this process should be tempered by the knowledge that the characteristics of each distant class will vary and that revisions required for one learner group may be inappropriate for a different student population.

Effective teachers use a variety of means, some formal and others informal, to determine how much and how well their students are learning. For example, to formally evaluate student learning, most teachers use quizzes, tests, examinations, term papers, lab reports, and homework. These formal evaluation techniques help the instructor to evaluate student achievement and assign grades. To evaluate classroom learning informally, teachers also use a variety of techniques. For example, teachers pose questions, listen carefully to student questions and comments, and monitor body language and facial expressions. Informal, often implicit evaluations permit the teacher to make adjustments in their teaching: to slow down or review material in response to questions, confusion, and misunderstandings; or to move on when student performance exceeds expectations.

When teaching at a distance, educators must address a different teaching challenge than when teaching in a traditional classroom. For example, instructors no longer have:

— A traditional, familiar classroom.

— A relatively homogeneous group of students.

— Face-to-face feedback during class (e.g. students' questions, comments, body language, and facial expressions).

— Total control over the distance delivery system.

— Convenient opportunities to talk to students individually.

For these reasons, distance educators may find it useful to not only formally evaluate students through testing and homework, but to use a more informal approach in collecting data to determine:

— Student comfort with the method used to deliver the distant instruction.

— Appropriateness of assignments.

— Clarity of course content.

— If class time is well spent.

— Teaching effectiveness.

— How a course can be improved.

Evaluation can be either formative, summative, or a combination of both.

Formative evaluation:

— Is an on-going process to be considered at all stages of instruction.

— Will enable the instructor to improve the course as he/she proceeds.

— Facilitates course and content adaptation.

— Will identify major gaps in the instructional plan or the need for minor adjustments.

Some strategies that educators can use to collect formative data from their distant students include:

— *Post cards* - provide each student with prestamped and preaddressed postcards. On a weekly basis, have students use the postcards to share their concerns or respond to questions during the last three to five minutes of class.

— *Electronic mail* - Can be a very effective way for instructors and students to communicate. Another plus, while the instructor is eliciting information about classroom learning, students become familiar with the use of electronic mail, a valuable skill.

— *Telephone* - Call students often. Ask them open ended questions (e.g., "What snags did you run into on the second writing assignment?") to let students voice their concerns. Follow with probes (e.g., "Then, will you need more information sources?"). Set phone-in office hours but be sure to welcome calls at other times.

Summative evaluation:

— Assesses overall effectiveness of the finished product or course.

— Can be a springboard in developing a revision plan.

— Can be a baseline of information for designing a new plan, program, or course.

— Will not help current students since it is conducted upon course completion.

Some questions that educators may want to ask students when collecting summative data include:

— List five weaknesses of the course.

— List three (or five) strengths of the course.

— If you were teaching the course, what would you do differently?

— Student background information: age, level in school, number of distance delivered courses taken prior to this one.

— What would you recommend to a friend planning to take this course?

— What did you think would be covered in this course but was not?

— Would you recommend this course to a friend? Why or why not?

Within the context of formative and summative evaluation, data may be collected through quantitative and qualitative methods.

Quantitative evaluation:

— Involves asking questions which can be statistically tabulated and analyzed, frequently using a scale, check list, or yes/no responses.

— Limits students to responding to the categories made available to them.

— Needs a large student sample for relevant statistical analyses.

Quantitative methods may be most useful for gathering information on large numbers of respondents for whom more in-depth, personalized approaches are not feasible. However, they do have some significant drawbacks:

— Many distance education courses have relatively small class sizes with students from various backgrounds. These small, stratified populations typically defy relevant statistical analysis.

— Quantitative surveys typically result in a rate of return of under 50 percent. A low rate of return often suggests that only those feeling very positively or negatively about the course responded to the evaluation.

— By definition and design, forced choice surveys offer respondents a limited number of possible response options. Therefore, fresh insights and unique perspectives falling outside the provided response categories go unreported.

— The cumbersome and often tedious nature of quantitative data collection can discourage formative evaluation, and often results in an over-reliance on summative evaluation.

— Statistical analysis often results in an illusion of precision that may be far from reality.

Qualitative evaluation:

— Is typically more subjective.

— Involves gathering a wider range and depth of information.

— Is more difficult to tabulate into neat categories.

— Will be less affected by typical small class size.

— Is a more flexible and dynamic method.

— Is not limited to pre-conceived topic of inquiry.

— Allows for student output of topics.

Qualitative evaluation can use:

— *Open ended questioning* — with respondents asked to identify course strengths and weaknesses, suggest changes, explore attitudes towards distance delivery methods, etc..

— *Participant observation* — with the distance educator observing group dynamics and behavior while participating in the class as an observer, asking occasional questions, and seeking insights regarding the process of distance education.

— *Non-participant observation* — with the distance educator observing a course (e.g., an audioconference, interactive television class, etc..) without actually participating or asking questions.

— *Content analysis* — with the evaluator using predetermined criteria to review course documents including the syllabus and instructional materials as well as student assignments and course-related planning documents.

— *Interviews* — with a facilitator or specially trained individual collecting evaluative data through one-on-one and small-group interviews with students.

The evalualtion areas should include:

— *Use of technology* - familiarity, concerns, problems, positive aspects, attitude toward technology.

— *Class formats* - effectiveness of lecture, discussion, question and answer; quality of questions or problems raised in class; encouragement given students to express themselves.

— *Class atmosphere* - conduciveness to student learning.

— *Quantity and quality of interaction* with other students and with instructor.

— *Course content* - relevancy, adequate body of knowledge, organization.

— *Assignments* - usefulness, degree of difficulty and time required, timeliness of feedback, readability level of print materials.

— *Tests* - frequency, relevancy, sufficient review, difficulty, feedback.

— *Support services* - facilitator, technology, library services, instructor availability.

— *Student achievement* - adequacy, appropriateness, timeliness, student involvement.

— *Student attitude* - attendance, assignments submitted, class participation.

— *Instructor* - contribution as discussion leader, effectiveness, organization, preparation,enthusiasm, openness to student views.

Instructional Tools

Instructional Television

Instructional television (ITV), is an effective distance education delivery system that can be integrated into the curriculum at three basic levels:

— *Single lesson* - Programs address one specific topic or concept, providing a lesson introduction, overview, or summary.

— *Selected unit* - A series of programs providing the content foundation for a learning unit in the course curriculum.

— *Full course* - Programs from one or more ITV series may be integrated into a full semester course typically in conjunction with instructional print materials.

ITV may be either passive or interactive. Passive ITV typically involves pre-produced programs which are distributed by video cassette or by video-based technologies such as broadcast, cable, or satellite. In contrast, interactive ITV provides opportunities for viewer interaction, either with a live instructor or a participating student site. For example, two-way television with two-way audio allows all students to view and interact with the teacher (see Lochte, 1993). At the same time, cameras at remote sites allow the teacher to view all participating students. It is also possible to configure the system so that all student sites may view one another.

Advantages

— Since most people have watched television, the medium is familiar.

— Motion and visuals can be combined in a single format so that complex or abstract concepts can be illustrated through visual simulation. The old cliche "a picture is worth a thousand words" rings true.

— Instructional television is an effective way to take students to new environments (the moon, a foreign country, or through the lens of a microscope).

— Time and space can be collapsed, so that events can be captured and relayed as they happen.

— It is very effective for introducing, summarizing, and reviewing concepts.

— It can be used effectively as a motivational tool.

Limitations

— Broadcast quality ITV is expensive to create.

— Video production is time consuming and can be technically demanding, often requiring relatively sophisticated production facilities and equipment.

— Sites choosing to interactively participate in an ITV program may require specialized equipment, facilities, and staffing.

— Most prepackaged ITV courses use a mass media approach to instruction aimed at the average student. As a result, they can be ineffective in serving students with special needs.

— When used passively, without interaction, its instructional effectiveness can be limited.

— Unless professionally produced, completed ITV programs often look amateurish.

— Once completed, ITV programs can be difficult to revise and update.

Designing instruction for ITV

In designing instruction for ITV, the challenge is to think in visual terms. Taking advantage of the visual imagery of ITV can counter an over-reliance on lecturing. Carefully planning ways to show instead of tell may improve the instructional effectiveness of ITV. It may be helpful to visually represent:

— Outlines or lists

— Key points

— Complex material in a step-by-step fashion

— Relationships

— Information that needs to be summarized for retention and recall

Make use of:

— Pictures — to show what things look like.

— *Diagrams* — to illustrate conceptual relationships, organizations, and structure of content material.

— *Maps* — to show spatial relationships.

— *Graphs, tables, and charts* — to summarize information.

Take advantage of video's ability to show movement to:

— Demonstrate the operation of tools and equipment.

— Demonstrate skills that learners are expected to emulate.

— Conduct experiments in which the processes must be observed.

— Analyze change over time using animation, slow motion, or time lapse photography.

— Reveal the spatial, three-dimensional qualities of an object or structure.

— Transport learners to places or situations not otherwise in their experience.

— Present primary source materials for analysis, such as film of historical events or naturally occurring situations.

Because teachers and students are physically separated by a distance, the teacher's challenge is to psychologically reduce the gap not only through the appropriate use of technology but also through the use of effective teaching practices. Good teaching ensures that a rapport develops between students and teacher. Once basic teaching methods are considered, try employing the following three step strategy for conducting ITV lessons: 1. Set the Stage

— Remember that it takes longer to deliver instruction at a distance than in a traditional face-to-face setting. Plan lessons accordingly.

— Practice in front of a live camera prior to class. If possible, have a colleague, a few target students, or a media technician view your presentation and on-camera presence, offering suggestions for improvement.

— Organize all class materials and visuals before the start of the class. It is best to have a trial run with technical staff so that all participants know the role they are expected to play.

— If using an overhead camera to electronically project visuals, understand its operation and limitations prior to the start of the class.

— Prepare viewers for new terminology to be used in the program, and answer any questions regarding the technical equipment being used, such as cameras, television monitors, audio equipment, etc..

— Inform students if there will be camera operators or technicians in the classroom. Although the students may be initially curious, this will fade as the class progresses. In-class technicians are trained to be as unobtrusive as possible.

— Students should have the necessary background materials to make the best use of televised lessons. Consider the use of study questions to assist in focusing discussions.

— Consider team teaching to maintain viewer interest with a change of voice, image, and presentation style. If using guest speakers, give students necessary background information prior to the class. Do the same for the guest speakers. Let them know the specific purpose of their session, what is expected of them, and the general background of participating students.

— Vary facial expressions, tone of voice, body movements, and eye contact with the camera to enhance verbal communication.

— Engage students by using humor, asking questions, involving students, and praising student contributions.

— Maintain energy and dynamism to attract and hold the distant learners' attention. Remember, enthusiasm is contagious. So is boredom.

— Present content in five to ten minute blocks interspersed with discussion. Alternate between instruction and interaction.

— Keep lecture sessions simple and clear. To help focus viewing, indicate key points to look for.

— Do not read material.

— Maintain a moderate speaking pace.

— Do not digress — keep students on track.

— Include different kinds of student involvement— watching, reading, writing, and talking.

— Vary the center of focus for activities from the on-camera presenter to a receive site group or individual.

— Incorporate timely breaks as a respite from the television monitor.

— Motivate peer learning and support by encouraging students to work together both in and out of class.

— Review the concepts discussed in the program and clarify any misunderstandings by asking focused questions.

— Integrate activities to reinforce the content presentation. These activities might include quizzes, worksheets, role-playing, and experiments.

— Planning a block of time for interaction and then letting students know in advance that interaction is anticipated. Initiating an interaction within the first twenty minutes will get students motivated to participate in learning rather than lulling them into just watching.

— Designating students at distant sites to lead discussions or survey the room for questions.

— Clearly defining discussion topics or questions and then allowing time for students to prepare responses. Assigning discussion questions in advance of the television session will help students prepare for the interaction. Have the questions appear in writing on the screen so students see and hear the questions.

— Encouraging student-to-student interaction by asking an in-class student or a student from a distant site to respond to questions. The instructor does not always have to answer questions.

— Functioning as content facilitator not just content provider.

— Review the taped recordings of the presentation, either with technical staff, a colleague, or by yourself. Take notes for improving presentation, style, and delivery methods.

— Seek student feedback on the strengths and weaknesses of the instructional materials and the teaching strategies being used.

— Be open to new ideas and delivery techniques for improving instructional effectiveness.

Interactive Videoconferencing

Interactive Videoconferencing (IV) is an effective tool that may be used in distance education settings. This system can be integrated into the distance education program with minimal adaptation to the curriculum and course and is designed to support two-way video and audio communication between multiple locations. Most IV systems utilize compressed digital video for the transmission of motion images over data networks such as high capacity Integrated Services Digital Networks (ISDN). The video compression process decreases the amount of data transmitted over the lines by transmitting only the changes in the picture. By minimizing the bandwidth required to transmit the images, video compression also reduces the transmission cost.

Interactive videoconferences are often transmitted on dedicated T-1 phone lines. These high speed lines are very effective for videoconferencing, but they are typically leased circuits with an expensive monthly cost. The fixed monthly charge is usually based on distance, not usage. Therefore, the cost effectiveness of IV systems increases with use. Interactive videoconferencing systems can operate at different data rates, at various fractions of T-1 capacity, enabling the transmission of multiple simultaneous videoconferences over the same T-1 circuit. An IV system can also share a T-1 circuit with other digital data uses such as Internet transmissions or file transfers.

Point-to-point

Interactive videoconferencing is commonly used to connect two locations using sophisticated computer technology. The core of IV is the codec (coder/decoder). This is the electronic device that transmits and receives the video signals that the class members will see on their television monitors. It may be easier to think of the codec as an extremely sophisticated modem. A modem takes digital data and transmits it over regular phone lines. The codec takes analog signals, compresses and digitizes them, and transmits the signals over digital phone lines. Other types of equipment, such as television monitors, are needed to make IV successful. In addition, various forms of instructional technology can be incorporated into IV, including video cassette recorders/players, microphones, cameras, and computers.

Point-to-Multipoint

Some systems are also capable of simultaneously connecting more than two sites through the use of a multi-point control unit, or MCU. Multi-point conferencing can be effective although the scheduling, technical, and logistical dimensions of MCU conferences can be imposing.

Dial Out Capability

A relatively new "dial out" feature, allows the use of multiple telephone lines to connect two or more sites in the same conference. Simultaneously accessing multiple lines may be difficult in small areas. In addition, the cost of the telephone line usage may be prohibitive since the cost of the call would be multiplied by the number of lines utilized in the conference.

Advantages

Interactive video can be effective because it:

- Allows "real time" visual contact between students and the instructor or among students at different sites.
- Supports the use of diverse media. Blackboards, handwritten documents, and videos may be incorporated at all sites.
- Enables connection with experts in other geographical locations.
- Can provide access to at-risk or special needs students.
- Provides additional access to students at remote sites.

Limitations

As with any technology, interactive video has its limitations:

- The initial cost of the equipment and leasing the lines to transmit conferences may be prohibitive.
- Companies which produce codecs have each developed unique methods of compression which are incompatible, although protocols have been established to allow communication among brand names. However, this "universal standard" compromises resolution and quality to a certain degree.
- Unless a strong effort is made by the instructor, students not located with the instructor may remain uninvolved in the course.

— If visuals, like handwritten or copied materials, are not properly prepared, students may have a difficult time reading them.
— If the "pipe" that carries the transmission among sites is not large enough, the students may observe "ghost images" when rapid movement occurs in "real time".
— If the system is not properly configured, class members may observe an audio "echo" effect. The result is audio interference that detracts from the learning environment.

Types of Videoconferencing Systems

— *Small room videoconferencing.* This system is designed primarily for small groups (1-12 participants) at all sites seated around a conference table.
— *Classroom videoconferencing.* This type of system usually uses high quality AV components, codecs, and an interface that allows all participants to be seen on the monitors.
— *Desktop videoconferencing.* This system utilizes a personal computer and videoconferencing software. These systems are less expensive, but offer limited resolution. They are most effective for individual and small group use.

Designing Instruction for Interactive Video

When designing instruction to be delivered over IV, the instructor should focus attention on all students, not just those at the "home" site. Lessons should incorporate a variety of activities for all students at the various sites. Use small group activities, student presentations, and an occasional break to add variety to the lesson. As a rule of thumb, instructors should change instruction methods every 10-15 minutes. In other words, switch from lecture to question-answer to small group activity on a regular basis. It is often helpful to bring guest lecturers into the classroom. It may also be helpful to have guest speakers at one or more of the distant sites. This will encourage involvement of the distant students, as well as allowing the students at the origination site to "see what it is like" to have the teacher at another location. When preparing class visuals, keep in mind that small fonts and light colors do not show up well over the monitors. A variety of formatting will also assist in maintaining student interest and attention. When formatting visuals, be sure that they will fit on the television monitor.

Instructional Strategies

— *Establish Class Expectations*: In the distance education classroom, some students may adopt the "TV" attitude, expecting the course to be entertaining, not educational. Address this attitude through well planned and focused presentations with emphasis on teacher-student interaction.

— Reduce Distractions: Students should also be forewarned to minimize extraneous noise and activity. Both detract from the quality of the course.

— *Use Variety and Interaction*: The instructor should begin the course by preparing the learners for an active experience. Interactive videoconferencing is interactive, unlike regular television, and students can make the class much more interesting by being actively involved.

— *Encourage Dialogue*: By asking questions and noting body language, instructors can ascertain the interest and comprehension of the students at both all sites. This kind of attention will make all students feel more comfortable.

— *Training for Instructors and Students*: It is important that an instructor be taught how to use all features of the equipment. A short session (30 minutes) should be sufficient to give the instructor a "hands-on" overview of the equipment features. It would also be helpful to provide the instructor with a quick reference sheet outlining major functions. Some of the critical operations that an instructor should be capable of performing are:

  — Turning on the codec and the monitors.

  — Dialing the distant site(s) to establish a link.

  — Controlling camera focus and field at the origination site and at the distant site(s).

  — Adjusting the volume to an acceptable level.

  — Dialing out to a remote location.

  — Selecting the appropriate data rate.

  — Re-setting "echo canceling" capability.

  — Switching to and from the document camera.

  — Switching to and from the computer output.

  — Utilizing a computer to generate and display multimedia presentations.

  — Using the VCR to broadcast a video for all locations.

  — Terminating the link with the distant site(s).

— Shutting down the equipment.

Some institutions have technicians who will assist the instructor in setting up or monitoring the videoconference. However, the instructor should still be aware of the process because the technician may not always be available. Student training may also be critical since they may be called upon to operate the equipment if the instructor is at another site, is unavailable, or if a guest speaker needs assistance. Interactive videoconferencing can be an effective instructional tool for the distance educator. As with other technologies, its usefulness is directly related to the instructor's understanding of its benefits, limitations, and utilization strategies.

Computers in Distance Education

Educators have witnessed the rapid development of computer networks, dramatic improvements in the processing power of personal computers, and striking advances in magnetic storage technology. These developments have made the computer a dynamic force in distance education, providing a new and interactive means of overcoming time and distance to reach learners. Computer applications for distance education fall into four broad categories:

— *Computer Assisted Instruction (CAI)* - uses the computer as a self-contained teaching machine to present discrete lessons to achieve specific but limited educational objectives. There are several CAI modes, including: drill and practice, tutorial, simulations and games, and problem-solving.

— *Computer Managed Instruction (CMI)* - uses the computer's branching, storage, and retrieval capabilities to organize instruction and track student records and progress. The instruction need not be delivered via computer, although often CAI (the instructional component) is combined with CMI.

— *Computer Mediated Communication (CMC)-* describes computer applications that facilitate communication. Examples include electronic mail, computer conferencing, and electronic bulletin boards.
— *Computer-Based Multimedia-* HyperCard, hypermedia, and a still-developing generation of powerful, sophisticated, and flexible computing tools have gained the attention of distance educators in recent years. The goal of computer-based multimedia is to integrate various voice, video, and computer technologies into a single, easily accessible delivery system.

Advantages

— Computers can facilitate self-paced learning. In the CAI mode, for example, computers individualize learning, while giving immediate reinforcement and feedback.
— Computers are a multimedia tool. With integrated graphic, print, audio, and video capabilities, computers can effectively link various technologies. Interactive video and CD-ROM technologies can be incorporated into computer-based instructional units, lessons, and learning environments.
— Computers are interactive. Microcomputer systems incorporating various software packages are extremely flexible and maximize learner control.

— Computer technology is rapidly advancing. Innovations are constantly emerging, while related costs drop. By understanding their present needs and future technical requirements, the cost-conscious educator can effectively navigate the volatile computer hardware and software market.

— Computers increase access. Local, regional, and national networks link resources and individuals, wherever they might be. In fact, many institutions now offer complete undergraduate and graduate programs relying almost exclusively on computer-based resources.

Limitations

— Computer networks are costly to develop. Although individual computers are relatively inexpensive and the computer hardware and software market is very competitive, it is still costly to develop instructional networks and purchase the system software to run them.

— The technology is changing rapidly. Computer technology evolves so quickly that the distant educator focused solely on innovation "not meeting tangible needs" will constantly change equipment in an effort to keep pace with the "latest" technical advancements.

— Widespread computer illiteracy still exists. While computers have been widely used since the 1960's, there are many who do not have access to computers or computer networks.

Students must be highly motivated and proficient in computer operation before they can successfully function in a computer-based distance learning environment.

Internet and Distance Education

The Internet is the largest, most powerful computer network in the world. It encompasses 1.3 million computers with Internet addresses that are used by up to 30 million people in more than fifty countries. As more and more colleges, universities, schools, companies, and private citizens connect to the Internet either through affiliations with regional not-for-profit networks or by subscribing to information services provided by for-profit companies, more possibilities are opened for distance educators to overcome time and distance to reach students. With access to the Internet, distance educators and their students can use:

— *Electronic mail (e-mail)* - Like postal mail, e-mail is used to exchange messages or other information with people. Instead of being delivered by the postal service to a postal address, e-mail is delivered by Internet software through a computer network to a computer address.

— *Bulletin boards* - Many bulletin boards can be accessed through the Internet. Two common public bulletin boards on the Internet are USENET and LISTSERV. USENET is a collection of thousands of topically organized newsgroups, covering everything from supercomputer design to bungee cord jumping, and ranging in distribution from the whole world to single institutions. LISTSERV also provides discussion forums on a variety of topics broken out by topic or area of special interest.

— *World-Wide Web (WWW)* -The WWW is an exciting and innovative front-end to the Internet. Officially WWW is described as a "...wide-area hypermedia information retrieval initiative aiming to give universal access to a large universe of documents". The WWW provides Internet users with a uniform and convenient means of accessing the wide variety of resources (pictures, text, data, sound, video) available on the Internet. Popular software interfaces, such as Mosaic and Netscape, facilitate navigation and use of the WWW. The central organizing feature of the WWW is the "home page". Every organization and even every individual user of the WWW can create a home page that contains whatever information they want to present. The hypertext capabilities of the WWW facilitate linking of information within your own home page and with all other home pages on the WWW.

Distance educators can use the Internet and WWW to help students gain a basic understanding of how to navigate and take full advantage of the networked world into which they will be graduating. Some instructional possibilities of the Internet include:

— Using e-mail for informal one-to-one correspondence. Feedback from the instructor can be received more quickly than messages sent by mail. Students can read messages at their convenience and easily store them for later reference.

— Establishing a classroom bulletin board. Distant students often work in isolation without the assistance and support of fellow students. Setting up a class bulletin board can encourage student-to-student interaction. With a class computer conference, individual students can post their comments or questions to the class, and every other individual is free to respond. The conference can also be used to post all modifications to the class schedule or curriculum, assignments/tests, and answers to assignments/tests.

— Engaging students in dialogue with other students, faculty, and researchers by encouraging them to join a bulletin board(s) on topic(s) related to the class.

— Developing a classroom home page. The home page can cover information about the class including the syllabus, exercises, literature references, and the instructor's biography. The instructor can also provide links to information on the WWW that would be useful to students in the class (e.g., real research data on agricultural markets, global climate change, or space missions). Other links could access library catalogs or each student's individual home page.

When incorporating the Internet into a distance delivered course, remember that:

— All students in a course must have Internet and WWW access to ensure equal opportunities for computer interaction and feedback. Also, convenient access to a computer at home or work may influence student success.

— Students may face the concurrent challenges of learning basic computer skills, new software, and appropriate online communication skills. Trouble-shooting student computer problems will probably become a part of normal instructional responsibilities. Setting up a specific classroom conference for ongoing discussions of specific hardware and software problems may help students to work through these problems on their own.

— Some students might hesitate to contribute to computer conferences or to send e-mail because of a lack of familiarity with the proper protocols. Encourage students to use e-mail, classroom conferences, electronic bulletin boards, and the WWW early in the course so they overcome inhibitions. Specifying a minimum number of e-mail communications per week will encourage active participation.

— Using e-mail can help the instructor provide feedback more quickly than surface mail or telephone. Prompt response generally increases student motivation and performance.

— Prompt responses might not always be appropriate. Computer conferences can foster student-to-student interaction. To ensure that this interaction is sustained, work towards a facilitative role. It might be appropriate to delay response to a query in a classroom conference in order to allow students to respond to the issue and to each other.

— Becoming familiar with the resources available on the Internet and the most effective ways to use them will be part of the instructional challenge. A number of helpful guides to the Internet and WWW are available.

Print in Distance Education

Print is the foundation of distance education and the basis from which all other delivery systems have evolved. The first distance-delivered courses were offered by correspondence study, with print materials sent and returned to students by mail. While technological developments have added to the repertoire of tools available to the distance educator, print continues to be a significant component of all distance education programs.

Advantages

— *Spontaneous.* Print materials can be used in any setting without the need for sophisticated presentation equipment.

— *Instructionally transparent.* The medium of delivery should enhance, not compete with, the content for the learner's attention. If the student reads well, the print medium is the most transparent instructional medium of all.

— *Non-threatening.* Reading is second nature to most students. As a result, they are easily able to focus on the content, without becoming mesmerized or frustrated by the process of reading itself.

— *Easy to use.* Given adequate light, print materials can be used any time and any place without the aid of supplemental resources such as electricity, viewing screen, and specially designed electronic classrooms. The portability of print is especially important for rural learners with limited access to advanced technology.

— *Easily reviewed and referenced.* Print materials are typically learner-controlled. As a result, the student rapidly moves through redundant sections, while focusing on areas demanding additional attention.

— *Cost-effective.* No instructional tool is less expensive to produce than print. In addition, facilities abound for the inexpensive duplication of these materials.

— *Easily edited and revised.* In comparison to technically sophisticated electronic software, print is both easy and inexpensive to edit and revise.

— *Time-effective.* When instructional print materials are created, the developer's primary focus remains on content concerns, not the technical requirements of the delivery system.

Limitations

— *Limited view of reality.* Print, by its reliance on the written word, offers a vicarious view of reality. Despite the use of excellent sequential illustrations or photos, for example, it is impossible to adequately recreate motion in print.

— *Passive and self-directed.* Numerous studies have shown that higher learner motivation is required to successfully complete print-based courses. To a certain extent, the passive nature of print can be offset by systematic instructional design that seeks to stimulate the passive learner. Still, it takes more motivation to read a book or work through a written exercise than it does to watch a television program or participate in an audioconference with an instructor encouraging student participation and response.

— *Feedback and interaction.* Without feedback and interaction, instruction suffers, regardless of the delivery system in use. By nature, print materials are passive and self-directed. Even with print materials incorporating feedback mechanisms and interactive exercises, it is easy for learners to skip to the answer section.

— *Dependent on reading skills.* Thanks to television, most students have developed fairly good viewing skills by age four. These same children, however, often fail to develop adequate reading skills by age 12. Reading skills must often be improved. Lack of ability in this area cripples the effectiveness of even the most instructionally sound print material and must be overcome if print is to be used effectively.

Formats of Print Materials

Various print formats are available, including:

— *Textbooks.* As in traditionally delivered courses, textbooks are the basis and primary source of content for the majority of distance-delivered courses. While textbooks should always be critically reviewed before adoption, this is especially critical when the learner and the instructor are not in daily contact.

— *Study guides.* Typically, distance educators use study guides to reinforce points made during class and through the use of other delivery systems. They will often include exercises, related readings and additional resources available to the student.

— *Workbooks.* In a distance education context workbooks are often used to provide course content in an interactive manner. A typical format might contain an overview, the content to be covered, one or more exercises or case studies to elaborate the points being made, and a quiz or test (with answer key) for self-assessment. In addition, there is typically some form of feedback, remediation, or "branching" loop to recycle students through the instruction as needed.

— *Course syllabus.* A comprehensive and well-planned course syllabus is the foundation of many distance-delivered courses. It provides course goals and objectives, performance expectations, descriptions of assignments, related readings (often by session), grading criteria, and a day-by-day overview of the material to be covered. The syllabus must be as complete as possible in order to guide the students through the course in the absence of daily contact with the instructor.

— *Case studies.* If written imaginatively, case studies are an extremely effective instructional tool. In fact, case studies are often designed around the limitations of print and intended to spark the students' imaginations as they place themselves in the particular case under consideration. Many case studies present a content-based scenario. They raise questions, pose alternative solutions, and then branch students to different sections of the text. There, the consequences of the selected alternative are described.

Designing Instruction for Print

Because print is largely a one-way communication medium, the challenge is to design instruction to maximize the amount of interaction in distance education print materials. Consider:

— Writing style. Misanchuk (1994) suggests that distance educators write instructional materials with language more like that used for speaking than for writing journal articles or books. His tips for writing instructional materials include:

— Use short sentences.

— Avoid compound sentences.

— Avoid excess information in a sentence.

— Use the active voice.

— Use personal pronouns.

— Keep equivalent items parallel.

— List conditions separately.

— Avoid multiple negatives.

— Use point form.

— Use familiar examples.

— Write as you would speak.

— Avoid unnecessary and difficult words.

— Avoid jargon; use technical terms only when necessary.

— Put sentences and paragraphs into a logical sequence: first things that affect many, then things that affect few; first the general, then the specific; first permanent provisions, then temporary ones.

— Avoid cultural and gender stereotyping.

— Focusing on content organization before developing content. Prior to content development, create an outline of the material to be covered. Print materials are often too wordy because the author is planning, organizing and writing at the same time. Instead, organize content based on the identified goals and objectives. At first, focus on systematically and creatively ordering the flow of topics, not polishing a finished product. The end result will be a well-organized content outline from which the written content will easily flow.

— Developing a course introduction. Misanchuk (1994) suggests developing a written course introduction that will be the very first thing a distant student sees. The course introduction can include biographical background information about the instructor, a course overview, course goals and aims, a listing of any textbooks or ancillary learning materials that will be needed, and information about assignments, examinations, and grading.

— Staying with a consistent format. Learner anxiety with the unknown can be reduced through consistency in instructional presentation. Develop an effective format and organizational scheme and stick with it. Use adequate headings and subheadings to visually guide the reader through the material.

— Using advance organizers. Advance organizers are a means to connect new material with a learner's prior knowledge and cognitive structure. They should be of a more general and abstract character than the learning matter that follows and help the learner to relate different parts and concepts of teaching material to each other. Place the most general and comprehensive ideas at the beginning of a lesson and progress to more structured and detailed information.

— Using examples and analogies. In a traditional classroom, teachers spontaneously provide examples and analogies to illustrate a point that students are having difficulty understanding. Because distant students and their teachers may not have this type of interaction, include lots of good examples and analogies in print-based materials. Be sure, however, that these examples address the various cultural groups, ages and experiences of the students.

— Including questions. Questions in print material can stimulate the learner to be more active and to deal more intensively with the learning matter. Use questions that aim at understanding rather than merely reproduction and memorization of facts.

— Adding a table of contents. A detailed table of contents can help the learner to quickly refer to the appropriate section.

— Incorporating a glossary of terms. A glossary summarizes all the new, often technical terminology encountered in a document. It may be helpful to delineate glossary entries in the instructional material by putting them in boldface type.

In developing or adapting distance instruction, the core content remains basically unchanged, although its presentation requires new strategies and additional preparation time. Suggestions for planning and organizing a distance delivered course include:

— Begin the course planning process by studying distance education research findings. There are several excellent research summaries available.

— Before developing something new, check and review existing materials for content and presentation ideas.

— Analyze the strengths and weaknesses of possible delivery approaches, in terms of learner needs and course requirements, before selecting a mix of instructional technology. Avoid technological solutions in search of instructional problems.

— Hands-on training with the technology of delivery is critical for both teacher and students. Consider a pre-class session in which the class meets informally using the delivery technology and learns about the roles and responsibilities of technical support staff.

— At the start of class initiate a frank discussion to set rules, guidelines, and standards. Once procedures have been established, consistently uphold them.

— Make sure each site is properly equipped with functional and accessible equipment. Provide a toll-free hotline for reporting and rectifying problems.

— If course materials are sent by mail, make sure they are received well before class begins. To help students keep materials organized, consider binding the syllabus, handouts, and other readings prior to distribution.

— Start off slowly with a manageable number of sites and students. The logistical difficulties of distant teaching increase with each additional site.

— Understand the strengths and weaknesses of the instructional delivery systems available to you (e.g., audio, video, data, and print) as well as the technical means by which they are delivered (e.g., satellite, microwave, fiber optic cable, etc.).

— To function effectively, students must quickly become comfortable with the nature of teaching and learning at a distance. Efforts should be made to adapt the delivery system to best motivate and meet the needs of the students, in terms of both content and preferred learning styles. Consider the following strategies for meeting students needs:

- — Make students aware of and comfortable with new patterns of communication to be used in the course.
- — Learn about students' backgrounds and experiences. Discussing the instructor's background and interests is equally important.
- — Be sensitive to different communication styles and varied cultural backgrounds. Remember, for example, that students may have different language skills, and that humor is culturally specific and won't be perceived the same way by all.
- — Remember that students must take an active role in the distance delivered course by independently taking responsibility for their learning.
- — Assist students in becoming familiar and comfortable with the delivery technology and prepare them to resolve the technical problems that will arise. Focus on joint problem solving, not placing blame for the occasional technical difficulty.
- — Be aware of students' needs in meeting standard university deadlines, despite the lag time often involved in rural mail delivery.

— Using effective interaction and feedback strategies will enable the instructor to identify and meet individual student needs while providing a forum for suggesting course improvements. To improve interaction and feedback, consider the following:

- — Integrate a variety of delivery systems for interaction and feedback, including one-on-one and conference calls, fax, electronic mail, video, and computer conferencing. When feasible, consider personal visits as well.

— Contact each site (or student) every week if possible, especially early in the course. Take note of students who don't participate during the first session, and contact them individually after class.

— Make detailed comments on written assignments, referring to additional sources for supplementary information. Return assignments without delay, using fax or electronic mail, if practical.

— Arrange telephone office hours using a toll-free number. Set evening hours if most of your students work during the day.

— Early in the course, require students to contact you and interact among themselves via electronic mail, so that they become comfortable with the process. Maintaining and sharing electronic journal entries can be very effective towards this end.

— Use pre-class study questions and advance organizers to encourage critical thinking and informed participation on the part of all learners. Realize that it will take time to improve poor communication patterns.

— Have students keep a journal of their thoughts and ideas regarding the course content, as well as their individual progress and other concerns. Have students submit journal entries frequently.

— Use pre-stamped and addressed postcards and out-of-class phone conferences for feedback regarding course content, relevancy, pace, delivery problems, and instructional concerns.

— Call on individual students to ensure that all participants have ample opportunity to interact. At the same time, politely but firmly discourage individual students or sites from monopolizing class time.

— Use an on-site facilitator to stimulate interaction when distant students are hesitant to ask questions or participate. In addition, the facilitator can act as your on site eyes and ears.

— For the most part, effective distance teaching requires enhancing existing skills, rather than developing new abilities. Pay special attention to the following:

— Develop strategies for student reinforcement, review, repetition, and remediation. Towards this end, one-on-one phone discussions and electronic mail communication can be especially effective.

— Realistically assess the amount of content that can be effectively delivered in the course. Because of the logistics involved, presenting content at a distance is usually more time consuming than presenting the same content in a traditional classroom setting.

— Diversify and pace course activities and avoid long lectures. Intersperse content presentations with discussions and student-centered exercises.

— Be aware that student participants will have different learning styles. Some will learn more easily in group settings, while others will excel when working independently. While the same is true in traditional classroom settings, preferred student learning styles may be more difficult to determine at a distance.

— Humanize the course by focusing on the students, not the delivery system.

— Consider providing a strong print component to supplement non-print materials.

— Use locally relevant case studies and examples as often as possible to assist students in understanding and applying course content.

— Be concise. Use short, cohesive statements and ask direct questions, realizing that technical linkages might increase the time it takes for students to respond.

— Personalize instructor involvement, realizing that distance teaching does not replace the value of face-to-face contact and small group interaction. If budget and time permit, teach at least one session from each site. Typically, the earlier in the course this is done, the better.

Multimedia use in Instruction

A multimedia educator is as simple and easy as being a print educator. Educational use of multimedia has been increasingly strained by its many technologies and this has created an ongoing problem. Integrating multimedia into lesson and unit plans has often meant selecting one or more different machines to play or to enable a communication form. Once instructors went beyond large charts, globes and pull-down maps, multimedia became much more costly, cumbersome, complicated and less reliable as machines were needed. Further, as many of these machines were expensive, they were not routinely placed in every classroom. Instead, someone needed to make a trip to a media center to obtain the machine, then set it up and adjust it, then return it when finished.

An educator might need one cart in the room for the VCR, one for the overhead, one for the record player, another for the stereo system with speakers and radio tuner, and another for the videodisc player and so forth. If a teacher wanted to create any of these media, even more and different expensive machinery was needed. This situation seriously taxes the time resources of a teacher and the financial resources of a school. From one perspective, this has been further complicated by the advent of personal computers which needed even more expensive projection systems for whole class use and were even more complicated and temperamental in situations where they had to be set up, sometimes connected to other multimedia devices and then returned. On top of all these options, something newer emerged, the multimedia Internet. Accepting that the old audio-visual agenda such as television and still images on overheads, though somewhat taxing, is still useful to teachers, why is computer-based Internet-delivered multimedia important? First of all, this new development transforms the current situation. One machine can 'play' each of these media, with the computer acting as media 'jukebox' to a district and Internet storage system of staggering capacity. Further, the same machine with different software applications can be used for the composition of all of these multimedia forms. This is a powerful new development.

Internet capable computers now provide the most cost-effective way to deliver or utilize an enormous and still rapidly growing base of free multimedia based material of great value to educational classroom activity. This includes all eight of the major multimedia forms: text, computer programming, still images, animation, video, audio, virtual reality and device controllers (e.g., sensors, telescopes, robots). That is, this includes the software files of multimedia editors such as Powerpoint, Hyperstudio, Premiere and virtual reality applications and more. Further, the Internet provides accessibility to the sound and video samples of a wide array of multimedia that are available for purchase which would never otherwise even be seen for consideration by the average classroom teacher. In curriculum, significant power belongs to those who can create it and extends to the degree that they do create it. Multimedia technologies today include the most powerful communication form in Western culture, notably motion pictures (e.g., film and television) and their related composition tools. Camcorders are readily available to students and teachers.

Digital video editors allow anyone to easily edit and assemble their own video. Some computer manufacturers are including video editors as a part of the basic application software sold with the computer. With these resources teachers can and will develop and maintain the rights to their own copyrighted video work. Web servers allow the teacher's classroom computer unprecedented power to share videoclip and other media knowledge over greater geographic range than an earth based satellite. Within seconds of activating the built-in web server of Macintosh and Windows operating systems, or downloading web server freeware from the Internet, any current Internet-capable computer workstation rivals the technical power and global reach of international magazine publishers, and radio and television broadcast stations. This is unprecedented educational power. It is worth re-emphasizing, that beyond becoming effective users of the multimedia based works of others, and international publishers of the work of students, educators can also become creators and composers. Through multimedia technologies educators can develop work tailored not to the commercial needs of Hollywood, but to the specific educational needs of the students in their classroom. Computer technology provides a curb-cut that simplifies and accelerates the development of localized multimedia-based curriculum. Further, without this composition knowledge, educators are unable to make the most of Federal "fair use" provisions of the copyright law for multimedia that allow educators to clip and snip images, videoclips and audioclips out of longer works for educational use. That is, multimedia provides ever greater cultural relevance. For the reason of cultural relevance if no other, educators also need to teach the creation of video and its other multimedia extensions as effectively as they teach the creation of writing. For reasons of professional practice, every teacher needs to become as comfortable composing video as they are composing text. Through such composition, new and popular avenues for imagination, creativity and fantasy emerge.

Every educator depends on some form of multimedia every day. These educational values of multimedia can be summarized as:

Metaphor or perspective	understand by comparison and contrast with different points of view as represented by different senses through different media
Variation	change that grabs and maintains attention
Awareness	sense what you have not previously known replacement for a sense or senses disabled greater cultural relevance

These reasons alone provide compelling need for multimedia curriculum integration. But other important agenda items have also emerged. When engaged in higher order skills such as comparison, analysis, inference and evaluation, the mind must carry out its problem processing in some symbol system. Academic skills with verbal language and math are but two important languages (media) for thought. Though interpersonal and intrapersonal intelligences are not relevant to multimedia use, other intelligences or languages of thought from Gardner's theory are: spatial, bodily kinesthetic, musical, and naturalist. Multimedia development supports and integrates well with this latter set of abilities. That is, multimedia not only extends cognitive range but often takes the thinker to new areas within which to range. Many sequences have been developed to provide a kind of scaffolding for the mind as its works through problems. Further, the different tools sets available for multimedia require sequences which are sometimes complex and relatively lengthy.

Computer-based multimedia provides a constant fall-back position of help files, wizards and assistants which teach about and guide the user along these sequences. These assisting resources can be aware of the user's context at the computer and keep prompts and lists always on call to keep development of a composition solution moving forward. That is, computer-based multimedia enables more complex thinking because of the cognitive based support such software routinely provides. Problems can also be seen as difficulties with a certain perspective. One of the most common ways to attack a problem is to change the perspective in some qualitative way. Multimedia capable teachers have a valuable means for enabling those changes. As composers of multimedia resources, teachers use change of perspective to meet the varied learning styles of different learners.

There are two general concerns that hold back the body politic from supporting greater integration of the technologies that have come after the creation of text. The first is the reasonable concern for proof. Is there researched evidence that its use is effective? A second concern is the idea that multimedia represents a specialized high-end technology above and beyond K-12 and even University campus norms for the use of computer resources. The first is a problem of science, the second a problem of perception. That we pay so little attention to the former may be the result ofstruggle with the latter. To the degree that relevance to the larger world beyond classroom education is important, in fact, multimedia capacity has become the cultural norm. Educational curriculum appears to have lost sight of the emphasis on multimedia in culture. It is the classroom that is the back of the pack anomaly. In reference to personal computer technology, multimedia capacity of some sort is generally an assumed feature of computers reaching the market beginning with 1997. Multimedia capacity has been a standard feature of Macintosh computers since 1984. Even more striking, multimedia forms of information have been the principal means of communication among a significant portion the world's population, with more news and information transferring between phone, radio, television and images than the written word, for a number of years.

Television in turn has dominated these other multimedia forms and the written word in terms of the number of hours school-aged children choose a particular medium. This is not to imply that teachers should promote television over the written word or other forms of communication. But video is just a prominent example of a powerful multimedia communication tool that teachers have historically not been empowered to compose with for their own purposes. Instead, teachers should have the capacity to compose with many media for educational needs as they see fit as they should with any medium that is heavily used by students. Funding sources must continue to expand the portion of the budget that provides for multimedia hardware, software and training and innovative pedogogy which incorporates it. Within education there are two classes of users of multimedia that need to be emphasized in weighing its relevance: teacher education programs around the country; and schools within range of student teacher population. The influence of focus here will have broad long term influence on the rest of the educational system. There is an international organization of teacher educators that use technology, SITE. SITE stands for the Society for Information Technology and Teacher Education. It is made up primarily of university faculty in teacher education programs, but also includes school district media specialists, private schools and interested teachers.

The several hundred folks who attended their international conference represent a broad spectrum of United States teacher education programs. It is clear from their presentations and papers, that multimedia is an integral part of the design, research, development and teaching concerns of many programs. To the degree that a college and school district is concerned about best of class and leadership with information technology, multimedia capacity and coursework is simply required. Multimedia capacity has provided a number of tangible and less tangible benefits. Capacity and production played a key role in citation for excellence in the quality of computer and information technology program by an

NCATE evaluation team. Capacity has led to the development of several web projects that heavily use multimedia. All of those immediate application to students (especially CROP) of which video training clips are an important part.

The degree to which area schools around University use multimedia is likely to extend over a wide range. Many schools make inadequate use of the multimedia resources that are already available, often because of lack of exposure and training by their teachers. Their situation is not because of lack of publications on multimedia education. In addition to numerous articles, book length works go back a number of years with a steady stream of new works also appearing. That have school districts winning state awards for their multimedia developments, indicates that training and education is certainly part of the solution. These public school efforts are generally led by media specialists and librarians who do have adequate training and awareness of what they can do with what they have, awareness of what they need to acquire and a district situation supportive of these information age efforts.

A quick example provides a typical situation of a school close to current standards for computer technology. At one of College's Professional Development Schools, in addition to a number of older systems that are multimedia capable, the building has a new computer lab with some fifteen computers with multimedia editing capability, including digital video editing. Their principal has attended evening graduate course on Multimedia Education from time to time, and the last time she attended she brought along an interested teacher as well. One of their goals is to do as other schools around the country have done, and create their own school newscast.

Students will shoot the video with their own existing camcorders, and edit the pieces on the computer. They will save this work to videotape and broadcast it over the building's close circuit cable TV system. Their training and knowledge however is inadequate to the task and we are in dialog over how to solve this problem. The College is fortunate in that its Instructional Technology Center has the hardware, software and trained lab assistants to manage a wide range of multimedia composition tools. But it lacks the outreach resources to significantly impact the schools in its region in this regard.

To educators that are highly dependent on text as the primary means of communication, it can be hard to accept the very powerful aspects of other media in culture. By its nature, the very use of other media competes with time for enhancing ones skills with the medium of text. Obsession with the medium of print and text however is self defeating. Text is enhanced if one accepts the inherent educational challenge to find ways to so meld all media that other media reinforce the value of text and its many efficiencies. We have accepted the value of this capacity without question with "early" readers, books that consist of primarily images with a touch of text. The goal must be to extend the metaphor of "early" readers to the full range of multimedia. As culture moves towards greater multicultural and multilingual requirements, so must communication evolve with greater facility with multimedia. With any powerful and creative force, there is also a dark side to its power. Under the guise of new technologies, old problems with sexuality, hate, truthfulness and more re-emerge, a problem which requires continual vigilance. Perhaps the most disturbing is the use of media to desensitize culture to violence. This occurs through not only the acceptance but the glorification of violence in movies, television and music. This development is further magnified by training children and adolescents to kill in realistic simulations during video arcade games. These games use forms of conditioning and training identical or very similar to those used in police and military training. Though educational research is inconclusive in this regard, it remains an issue deserving further attention. Through the critique of such "curriculum materials" provided byculture, through political lobbying and more, through an understanding of the psychology by which killing is enabled, educators must work strenuously to defang this significant and dangerous use of new media.

As the web (the Internet) acquired the power to share such media forms, the computer gained global publishing power. As the web merges every prior medium, new-age composers will incorporate the full range of metaphor, variation and awareness in one presentation space, with one machine. The computer has become the universal reader. The computer has also become the universal writer. The web page has become the universal form for communication. But the integration is even tighter than the mere parallel display of text, sound and image on one web page. These elements interact. Within the same web page, a click on text changes adjacent video display. Video display can change text either called automatically as the video plays or with a click within the video display area. Each form can control the timing and display of the other. It is no more proper to think of this as multimedia than it is to think of writing as multi-speech. There is a new level of integration. It is not too far-fetched to conclude that the web-based medium will dominate all prior medium in the twenty-first century.

It is worth pausing to let the import of that thought sink in more deeply. Though the Internet began as a text-only communication system, in the last few years it has matured as an important multimedia publication medium for all the technologies of human communication. Though still in its infancy this medium already provides even individuals with a broadcast range that surpasses all prior technologies in human history. In the technology research labs the quality of display is already as high or higher than all prior technologies for all media. Further, the form factor for the display of this media is greater than all prior technologies, from screens in research labs that turn and twist in all the sizes and flexibility of paper to functioning stadium size video walls. New generations of communicators must compose for this new world. In contrast with the integrating nature of this medium, education of learners for the emerging world of web composition is fractured, incomplete and balkanized. This is true from elementary school through university graduate programs. As members and participants in educational system, we have an obligation to organize and develop the merging of all prior communication skills.

An opportunity to develop a school of holistic composition. Though the web term of 'linking' is cognitively the shortest term to express the technical aspects of integrating multimedia, linking is insufficient to express the deeper power that it contains. Others promote the term uni-media as a label for this deep integration, though this term is somewhat ambiguous. The phrase comprehensive composition is another offering as a phrase to replace the reign of the term multimedia and less awkward than the holistic composition phrase. Comprehensive composition involves the planned integration and design of multiple units or forms of communication. At one level it parallels the mechanical skills required in reading (transposition of of written characters into thought) and writing (transfer of thought into written characters). More importantly, linking is open to and parallels the more advanced reflection and organization required of larger structures such as essays, books, and movies. Future curriculum for 21st century learners must consist of reading, writing and linking a range of multimedia elements.

The cultural importance of this transition parallels the magnitude of change initiated by the move thousands of years ago from oral to written culture. With time, reading and writing gained an aura that is represented by the vast depth and range of the content of today's libraries. With time, a similar development will happen with comprehensive composition. How vast is the opportunity for educational and cultural change before us? Imagine a world in which each of the primary and secondary colors is taught as a separate content or subject area, courses which separately study the expression and composition of shades of each of these six colors. In this world, each color has a deep tradition of study and expression that extends back decades and in some case centuries. Then, suddenly, someone discovered that these six colors could be mixed to create new colors, and that the concept of mixing colors on one canvas was born. New works of millions of combinations that had never been seen would have emerged. Such is the state of education for composition today. The web is the new canvas upon which new works of integration are being wrought.

In the university environment the study of different forms of composition is fractured into different colleges and schools. Written composition 'belongs' to the English department. Radio, television and theater composition belongs to communication arts. Image creation from canvas to photography belongs to the art department. Music belongs to the music department. Yet one web page can contain all these elements and more in interaction with each other. Some skills are still not part of the regular curriculum for all students even if in college, such as radio and television. Other skills are not even a part of the university agenda. For example, many institutions have not even one course in any program devoted to virtual reality development. Such offerings in K-12 public schools too often depend solely on the random interests of individual teachers. Rare is the person with the confidence to paint with the full palette of media colors let alone the confidence to teach others to paint with this range of expression. Nothing said here should be taken to imply that acquiring multimedia composition and linking skills is simple, that is just a matter of an another semester length course. Learning these skills is the equivalent complexity of learning to read and write, skills educational system spreads over ten or more years.

As basic reading ability can be grasped relatively quickly but sophisticated use takes a dozen years or more, so it is with multimedia. But it must be said that for the first time, the basic knowledge and tools are within the grasp of even primary level students who are given sufficient time and education with these technologies. Never has such power to communicate and express been put within reach of so many teachers and learners through computer based technology. No one can put an idea in-context better than front-line teachers in the classroom or learners using multimedia to construct meaning as they progress. This is an opportunity that deserves to be advanced. Numerous administrative challenges arise in considering such a concept. Should all composition classes be part of a vast new multimedia program? How would such a degree work if composition programs of study and faculty were to stay in different departments in K-12 and beyond? How will the infrastructure of multimedia and its delivery network be supported? To be empowered to compose requires many types of peripherals which input data into a multimedia capable computer, e.g., scanners, camcorders, videotape deck, television, microphones, and camera stands.

Computer technology provides the easiest, fastest and in many cases the least expensive way to create audio-video materials. The software is easy enough that students as well as teachers can and do create professional quality work. The most recent generations of computer technology have the capacity to become superb multimedia display systems, played from the massive storage of CD-ROMs such as multimedia encyclopedias or downloaded from the gargantuan and still radically expanding resources of the Internet. But even more valuable, personal computers can have the facility to digitize any media and then to compose, transpose, edit and publish, moving the multimedia material from the computer to slide, videotape, audiotape, CD-ROM disc, floppy disk and more. Comprehensive composition has practical benefits as well. This facility to invent with computer-based multimedia allows you to put multimedia needs in the local context, in the context of the learner, and in the display formats available to them. Increasing ease of use allows the youngest of learners to become composers, finders and editors for their own linking needs as well as allow teachers and administrators to do the same.

Preservice and inservice evaluation forms routinely include instructional variation as one of the important factors in assessing the quality of teaching. More recently different states, notably North Carolina, have required multimedia knowledge and skills as a part of the preservice licensure program. In addition to all these professionally serious concerns, many find multimedia development motivational and renewing. The elements of multimedia linking are a great source of fun, inspiration and creativity.

Multimedia is important to aspects of teaching, learning and problem solving including higher order thinking and multiple intelligences. Culturally multimedia represents significant forms of communication within Western culture. Within the education culture, school districts and colleges of education have demonstrated a recognition of its relevance through its inclusion in facilities and curriculum. It should also be noted that state and national educational standards require multimedia resources, skills and knowledge. Computer-based Internet delivered multimedia is the most cost-effective advertising and distribution system for multimedia that is available. Further, computer technology provides curb-cuts for multimedia that simplify its creation and development. Also, multimedia delivers important teaching and learning values: metaphor, variation and awareness. Most important of all, these three conceptual values and the full range of today's multimedia technologies merge together to provide opportunity for a new form of human communication. They add another giant new category to the concepts of reading and writing. They enable the newest power of the information age, the concept of comprehensive composition.

4

Open Learning: An Analysis

In many different places in the world today, students have the opportunity to create new knowledge and understandings by bringing their own unique perspective to local phenomena and information. Once the principal source of wealth was natural resources. Then it was mass production. The problem-solving capacity of the human mind—making products and tailoring services to the needs of people all across the globe.

The changing nature of the world's economic system--the shift from an industry based society to an information-based society—is a pervasive factor driving educational changes for people of all ages.

Society is shifting to the application of knowledge as the primary means of raising productivity. In an information-based society, knowledge work is the primary mode of work, since information provides the primary means by which work is accomplished.

Effective knowledge workers need to develop new higher-level skills for accessing, selecting, manipulating, and representing information in a variety of formats. But this alone is not sufficient. That vision of a quarter-century ago is now reality. We are facing the challenge of large-scale knowledge production. Workers at every stage or level of a knowledge-based organization must contribute to the production of knowledge.

In US, students and teachers contributing to the National Information Infrastructure (NII) by producing authentic products that represent their growing skills and knowledge. Collaborative inquiry in networked communities is a genre of learning, teaching, and knowledge-creating activity that illustrates many elements of educational reform and the knowledge-based society.

Students in schools around the nation and the world gather data from their local environments, such as acidity of their rain water, quality of the indoor air, ozone levels, water quality in rivers and streams, biological indicators of changes in climate or pollution, effects of ultraviolet light on plant and animal life, species diversity, wildlife populations, and migration patterns. They work in teams, often engaging parents and other local community members (such as scientists or engineers from a local water department) in their investigations. Each team is also part of a virtual community of scientists, students, and teachers in other schools.

Each school contributes to a collective database that includes information from many different geographic locations. Through the networks, the students work together to aggregate, analyze, and interpret the data and share their discoveries and interpretations. The large database gives students the opportunity to recognize geographic patterns in the data and provides a basis for comparing local data with data from other locations; data gathered locally now have more value because it is shared with a geographically distributed community. There are hundreds of such collaborative inquiry projects and communities organized by teachers, experts, and students.

In these kinds of collaborative inquiry communities, the learner has a real and responsive audience. This is highly motivating, just as it is motivating to any professional to get feedback from colleagues or audiences. The beneficial effects of this motivational aspect on learning have been studied in a systematic way by educational researchers.

Over the past several years, teachers and researchers have begun developing tools and standard methods that help make virtual communities more productive. In the Global Lab project organized by TERC, teachers, high school students, and research scientists around the world study local and global ecological change. They use low-cost instruments and sensors such as ozonometers, ion-selective probes for soil and water monitoring, and field data loggers.

To make meaningful scientific comparisons with sites from around the world, students and teachers must ensure that all factors influencing measurements are identical; when students in Moscow and Boston establish uniform guidelines to compare data, they learn the rigors and excitement of research. Students learn to investigate trends, compare their findings with local regulations and standards, and report and analyze data.

The use of common instruments and software helps establish a common basis for collaboration. A peer review system, access to scientists for online assistance, and participation in collaborative research groups help develop quality research projects. Much work needs to be done in establishing mechanisms for maintaining quality of the knowledge produced. Because they are located all over the world, schoolchildren can often monitor many more sites for environmental studies than the professional scientific community could support. This is the basic idea of the GLOBE project initiated by Vice President Gore.

Eventually, when large numbers of students and teachers have the appropriate tools, skills, and network participation, they will fill an important role in areas such as monitoring atmospheric ozone, ultraviolet light, water pollution, soil pollution, and bioindicators of global, regional, and local change.

The economic value of students' work has already been recognized by some of the companies that produce instruments and sensors. These companies value data collected in diverse circumstances and locations for testing their products; the companies provide the products to the community at reduced prices. Such networked educational projects sometimes have direct and concrete benefits to the local school and neighborhood.

One example is the series of air quality studies conducted by Global Lab students in Pease Middle School in San Antonio, Texas, which resulted in improvements to the ventilation system of the school and a new appreciation by parents and administrators of the contributions their young people can make. In US, school children's data on water quality have been of such utility to the town that banks and the Chamber of Commerce have established low- cost loans for parents to purchase computers for children, and companies are offering jobs for students to earn their own computers.

At Gonzaga High School in Washington D.C., students and their teachers are creating an Internet World Wide Web server on the subject of earth system science. Students use systems modeling software, data visualization tools (NCSA Image and NCSA Collage), and data from NASA databases to research earth system science topics.

In each project, the students conduct background research, create hypotheses, develop a strategy for data search, investigation, and testing, model the system qualitatively and quantitatively, and communicate their findings through a hypermedia document using NCSA Mosaic on the Internet. The teachers, Mike Keeler and Farzad Mahootian, are collaborating with teachers in other D.C. schools to form an exchange of such models and course materials through their Internet server.

The following characteristics of active learning provide a foundation for a participatory vision of education:

— bringing learning into a closer relationship to the real-world context of problems and projects;

— working collaboratively with peers and mentors;

— engendering closer relationships between people inside schools and outside in the "real world";

— working in a hands-on mode with the physical world, in addition to working with symbols and words;

— learning something just at the time it is needed to solve a problem or complete a project, rather than in a preset curriculum sequence;

— learning in an interdisciplinary context, rather than always separating subjects into isolated topics;

— working on a problem in depth, rather than covering many topics superficially;

— for teachers, becoming guides and mentors and learners, too, rather than only dispensers of knowledge;

— constructing one's own knowledge rather than memorizing facts from authorities;

— working on projects and problems of intrinsic interest to the learner or a group of learners, rather than learning what everyone else of the same age is expected to learn at the time;

— building learning experiences on the learning one does throughout life,

— rather than only on "school" subjects;

— basing assessment on performance of real tasks rather than on artificial tests;

— using the real tools for intellectual work that are used in the workplace, rather than oversimplified textbook techniques; and

— working directly with people from other places and cultures, rather than only learning about other places indirectly through books.

Creating this kind of foundation will be a collaborative effort or partnership among administrators, university faculty members, community, business, labor, and political leaders, as well as parents, teachers, and students.

The central value of internetworking to support learning and teaching for our changing world is that internetworking can support or enable authentic learning experiences and cross-institutional collaborations needed for the reform of education. When learners and teachers contribute to the information infrastructure by participating in virtual communities and by setting up information services on the networks.

The key characteristic of internetworking that enables this kind of experience is that the people who use the Internet are creating and exchanging knowledge, rather than passively receiving someone else's information. There is a danger that the networks could be used to transmit and amplify traditional and outmoded elements of schooling instead of providing a mechanism for the transformation to lifelong learning needed by all citizens.

Many well-intentioned efforts to apply technologies to schooling (often in the name of "reform") still assume such factory-era constraints as segregation of learners by age, a sequential curriculum, an emphasis on everyone learning the same thing at the same time, learning activities confined to the school or classroom, no participation of parents in the learning activities of their children, knowledge predigested by experts, teacher as authoritative knowledge base, memorization of facts today for use in later years, subjects isolated by disciplines, same roles for all teachers, right answers to all test questions, students following procedures written by outside authorities, class periods too short to think in, teachers as the only audience for students' work, and abstractions separated from experiential context.

How we shape and engineer the technology, tools, organization of knowledge, and virtual communities on the expanding Internet information infrastructure will directly affect the potential productivity, roles, and equity of opportunity of young people in the near and distant future, and thereby will affect the kind of society into which we evolve. These examples of learner and teacher contributions to the current Internet provide a glimpse of what is possible with today's technology, infrastructure, and organizational arrangements.

However, the value that people can contribute and the value that they get is limited by the local networking infrastructure, tools, and services on the Internet, and by the free-for-all nature of the interactions on most current virtual communities. Most contributions wind up as flotsam and jetsam on a vast chaotic sea of e-mail, newsgroup messages, and Web pages--with little order, discipline, quality assessment, structure, retrievability, review, or aggregation.

There has been considerable recent progress in developing software that makes it easier to get onto the networks and discover information from personal computers. As more people attempt to participate and more virtual communities are formed, we are gaining more insight into the kinds of tools and services needed for full participation, including user construction of knowledge and information services.

The Clinton-Gore Administration's National Information Infrastructure plan recognizes the importance of broad-based participation in the development of the Internet and the evolving nature of the NII: [T]he NII will be of maximum value to users if it is sufficiently "open" and interactive so that users can develop new services and applications or exchange information among themselves, without waiting for services to be offered by the firms that operate the NII. In this way, users will develop new "electronic communities" and share knowledge and experiences that can improve the way that they learn, work, play, and participate in the American democracy.

In US, the National School Network Testbed, BBN is collaborating with over 100 organizations that are exploring models for leveraging Internet access for educational innovation. This research has made it clear that scaling up is not a simple matter of physically connecting more people and organizations to the Internet.

If internetworking and the National Information Infrastructure are to support the transformation outlined here, then "scaling up" has to mean all these things, and more. Decisions made by government agencies, corporations, and communities about investment in infrastructure and educational reform will take into account the mechanisms needed to make progress on all of these fronts.

The pace of change is too fast for individuals to depend totally on others to structure their learning and information for them; pre-planned courses, textbooks, teacher training programs, technical support staff, and the like may not always be available to meet an individual's particular learning need. New curriculum frameworks, instructional materials, assessment and testing schemes, and teacher training programs will take into account these increased responsibilities for information management and knowledge creation.

Similarly, software and networked information services for educational purposes will be designed with the assumption that people will be taking on these responsibilities. For example, "ease of use" is a commonly requested characteristic of networks, information services, and software, but there is always a trade-off to be made between ease of use and complexity or functionality.

In the quest for ease of use of information and tools in the Internet, we must be careful not to exclude people from participating in the more complex and rewarding tasks of constructing knowledge. Students will learn how to deal with phenomena that are new and more complex than they are "ready" for, and will have opportunities to make sense out of situations before they understand all the first principles. Responsibility for teaching and mentoring will be shared more widely than in the past.

Classroom teachers will not be expected to have expertise in all the areas of knowledge their students are encountering. The communications networks will support teaching by people whose primary work is not formally teaching, but who have expertise in industry and other public sectors. Incentives to perform these part-time and out-of- school teaching and mentoring roles will be devised.

Communities and school districts making an investment in new curricula or technology should not attempt to overlay such innovations on outmoded methods of operation of schools; rather, they will look broadly for new opportunities to engage people in nontraditional roles. Learning is seen more as a process. Intelligence is recognized as diversified, and authentic assessment tells us to look at it in context.

Teachers and administrators are also learners. In that role they are typical learning organization managers. They are mentors; they guide, provide access to resources, facilitate. School itself is a more integrated system. School is divided into smaller clusters, where teachers and students and their families get to know one another and form a sense of community.

Collaborative groups work on meaningful projects, and just-in-time seminars and workshops provide support for the projects. Educational reforms will evolve in synchrony with the evolving information infrastructure. As a society, we are working hard on educational reform at the same time that we are evolving a new information infrastructure. There is a danger that the enormous efforts now put into educational "reforms" will turn out to be irrelevant to the circumstances of learning and working in a networked, knowledge-creating society.

Current investments in reformed curriculum frameworks, standards, assessments, teacher in-service programs, and the like should take advantage of networking to reduce industrial-age constraints; at the same time, they can contribute vitally to the evolving information infrastructure to the learning benefit of everyone.

Internet and the Humanities

Current developments in communication technology now provide new options for students to extend themselves across distances and through time. This technology invites children to leap off the "shoulders of giants" onto satellites and use this global perspective to participate in new ways with their peers and other experts in distant locations.

Classrooms are places where children learn the tools and skills necessary to be productive members of the society. Quality public education is the best form of national security a democracy can have. Children need to understand the value of freedom and diversity and to recognize the problems of tyrannies and dictatorships.

The stability of our democracy depends on children developing the skills for separating fact from fiction, theory from speculation, and information from propaganda. The decisions as to what to teach, who should teach, and how to teach are extremely complex and dynamic. We want children to have open access to multiple sources of information, but we also want them to have accurate, clear, and concise materials.

State agencies, as well as intellectual disciplines, create guidelines or frameworks for what should be part of the school curriculum. Teacher education programs and state certification procedures provide one way of regulating who will teach, at least in publicly funded schools.

The modes of instruction remain a hybrid of art and science, individual talent, and methods instruction. So each of these decisions is made by a complex partnership among the student, parents, teachers, schools, communities, districts, states, regions, and nations. In the information age, students with internet access can explore extensive libraries and international resources of materials in the humanities and social sciences. School libraries will effectively have an interlibrary loan program that will sweep the globe and be able to make vast amounts of information available instantly.

The networks provide more flexible and less intrusive ways for people to interact at a distance. For example, compare the PBS Online Newshour on the Internet, with their televised programs. In the broadcast version there is a tightly scripted sequence with limited time for all of the information collected.

In the online environment, much more information is available and the pace, order and content is up to the teacher or student. This extensive information source may make it easier to teach some subjects as both students and teachers will be able to find information which is not now available at their schools. However, the decisions about what to teach, with what methods and by whom are made by groups of people and not by giving schools extensive source materials. New forms of communication do encourage flexible partnership among those who create instructional materials and those who decide what is the subject to be taught .

In the future, the teacher is no longer alone in the classroom. There are mentors in the community and teachers and peers far away that are a part of the classroom activity. Students take more responsibility for their learning. The products of student work, such as the multi-media report on the pyramids, can become learning tools for peers in other locations.

A few educational projects are finding a large enough group of volunteers, but the numbers will not scale to cover all schools or all students. To create this level of partnership in schools would require a more organized approach. To achieve this vision, we will need to find ways of making these types of human resources available to students and teachers.

From this pool students and teachers could look for mentors. These experts may not hear from anyone during their period of service and unlike jury duty, they do not need to report to a location and spend the time waiting. If a person is selected as a mentor, as with jury duty, companies would be asked to donate their employee's time for a longer period of time to work with a student or student group. This would never constitute a full-time commitment as sitting on a jury does, but would be considered a legitimate activity within the work day.

There are undoubtedly citizens who would enjoy the opportunity to teach students about their work. This model could change the meaning of public education from one of public funding to one of public participation. If more people are involved with students, they become additional voices in the design of educational activities. They become more active partners in the dynamic process of deciding who teaches what to whom, and in what way. Distant students are already serving as educators in ways very similar to the example above, in which Egyptian students create a presentation for their partners.

Most teachers and students who work with distant peers expect to find out more about distant places; they are looking forward to contributions of the distant students as teachers. But in fact, the most important learning that teachers observe and students comment on from these collaborative projects is that of self-reflection. Working with distant students provides a mirror that reflects how one's own community defines who a person is and what he or she does that is unique.

The task of describing oneself to others and accepting the role of local expert is a very powerful way to develop self-knowledge and an understanding of one's own community. These observations lead to the next topic, the way in which networks help students leave the classroom and provide resources to the community and how these experiences lead to changes in education.

Computer and printer technology made it possible for people other than parents and teachers to easily read the products of young writers. Networks like the Internet, give students a world-wide distribution channel for their work and make it possible for them to share their work with other learners of all ages.

Students are much more willing to invest time when they are creating a library of materials that may be used by students anywhere in the world. Given the cost of developing materials, curriculum experts can cover only the major topics that most likely to be used by large number of classroom teachers. The packaged materials are expensive to create and produce. With the distribution channels of the Internet, however, it is possible to index and preserve many more topics.

This scenario of students creating learning tools for peers is only one of the many ways that students can reach out beyond classroom practice. Perhaps a few examples will demonstrate how electronically facilitated work could make it feasible for students to take a more active role in their community. Student voices are often missing in attempts to solve problems that directly involve them. In the '60's the common refrain was "If you are not part of the solution, then you are part of the problem."

Students are part of many problems and inviting them to part of the solution would, in itself, be a positive way of dealing with a host of social problems. Students could electronically serve on local, state, national, or world panels exploring social or global problems. Students might offer some clear insights and innovative ways of dealing with the complexity of problems that surround gangs, teen pregnancies, drug dependency, unemploymen$, and drunk driving. Schools could develop apprenticeship relationships with many different organizations.

For example, a news reporter might develop a column in the local newspaper that reports the ideas and thoughts of teenagers on a range of issues. The reporter could electronically send out a topic to schools for students to address, collect comments and writing from students around the city, then create a column that uses their ideas, words or suggestions. The list of contributing students could be part of the credits.

Students would be more likely to read the local newspaper if they knew that they might find their words, or those of their friends included in an article. Or students could serve as consultants to social agencies trying to provide find solutions to difficult problems. They could offer their solutions for anonymous but real social conflicts between parents and kids.

Students could take an active role in city planning decisions. When city parks, playgrounds, or walkways are planned, students could use these opportunities to work with models on the computers. They could interview citizens about their use of parks and playgrounds, discuss constraints with city planners and review budgets and costs of different materials to help formulate alternate plans for design.

Such a project would involve interpersonal skills, reading, writing, numerical computations, artistic design, and problem solving. Moving beyond the humanities into the sciences, one can identify many current projects in which students work with scientists to collect acid rain or weather measurements. The more involved students are in their communities, the less likely they are to feel the need to create their own counterculture gangs.

The fact is, technology does not change anything. The consistent theme is that people working together can create new solutions to old problems. Technology increases the number and range of people with whom we can easily interact, and it is these partnerships that lead to new forms of teaching and learning. The two scenarios provided a positive image of the use of technology in classrooms. Most advancements in human technology have their dark side.

Textbook descriptions reflect the view of dominant groups rather than an impartial record of the past. This mediated control of the view of history as well as the understanding or interpretation of all aspects of our culture is threatened by open access to materials on the Internet. Classroom access to distributed networks like the Internet brings these decisions to the classroom level and makes the student and teacher more active partners in deciding what content should be included.

Open and free access to all materials places children in the role of making decisions about relative truths. It makes it necessary for even very young children to understand the principles and problems of an open democracy. A tension exists between the desire to preserve free speech, a free press, and open access to information on one hand, and the need to help young children recognize and reject materials that preach hate and humiliation of individuals or groups on the other hand.

Networks are new forms of information distribution. They allow a greater participation in public dialog. In doing so, they raise old issues of public decency versus freedom of expression, of truth versus libel. And for schools, they highlight the need to rethink how society will make decisions about what is taught, by whom, and in what way. A similar problem arises with the use of mentors.

Teachers are certified and screened and yet every newspaper in every community reports stories about local teachers who abuse their close relationship with children. This also could be a problem with mentors. Those who want contact with children for illegal or immoral purposes may find mentor programs an easy way to find and interact with students. These are human problems that have been faced by each generation and will be solved by each generation in ways appropriate to changing times.

The doors of the Internet cannot be closed, but we can and are finding the ways to make sure that those we invite into the classroom and the materials that we make available to students help them develop the skills that they will need as adults. And one of these skills will be to recognize danger in cyberspace and learn how to avoid it.

Students are great inventors, writers, producers, musicians, and performers. The community, school, teacher, and student are all recognized in public forums such as newspapers and ceremonies. Sometimes there is prize money for the student only, sometimes the teacher or the school receives a reward and sometimes it involves a combination. Students are also creating print and online documents for community and for commercial services.

The construction and maintenance of a Web site might be an educational experience, but it is also a commercial service. Companies might "reward" the school with donation of equipment of access to other services. If we forge stronger links between the community and schools, these infrequent events may become more common. Rewarding student, teacher, or school could import many of the problems of the industrial age to the information age. It is possible to conceive of a school in which teaching acquires a monetary incentive.

School topics could be influenced by the availability of prize money or community contributions for services rendered. The decision of what to teach could be subverted by economic needs rather than intellectual development of the student. Students could become the information age workforce, with profit incentives driving education. These human problems are not new.

Technology does not change schools, people do. New opportunities and the ability to forge new partnerships bring with them new decisions. We should use the technology to help us think about these issues and come to terms with their evolution. No human problem can be solved for all time, since change is part of the human condition. As society changes, so will the way people interact with each other and with its tools.

Flexible short-term tele-apprenticeships can help students contextualize the skills they learn in school. The Internet may provide for a new structure of team teaching where many more people in the society play significant roles in education. Many students find classroom work meaningless and do not attend either intellectually or physically.

We have the tools to engage students in work that can be of use to the community. They can learn while participating in activities that have value to others. With new power tools come new dangers. It is important to explore the dangers and then develop the best safeguards possible. Understanding and dealing with ethical and moral issues associated with technology is an ongoing process that faces not only schools, but all sector of the society.

5

Open Learning Communities

The information and communication technologies (ICTs), dramatically expand our options for engaging in teaching and learning at the individual, community, and societal levels. ICTs provide opportunities for greater flexibility, interactivity and accessibility. They help visualize applications such as interactive radio and television, videoconferencing, teletext, Internet-based environments of dialogue, web publishing, and individualized CD-ROM tutorials.

We are at the edge of something potentially very exciting, extremely big and, quite frankly, truly overwhelming. Discussion around these new technologies thus tends to stir up a whole range of emotions ranging from optimism and hope to uneasiness and anxiety. The reason for this is that, in addition to expanding current delivery options, the emergence of these new technologies present us with the opportunity to question fundamental assumptions, to re-think existing approaches, to collectively conceptualize and generate new ideas and community-based alternatives and even sometimes, albeit more rarely, to catalyze social and institutional change. However, to unlock the potential of such technologies, it is critical to revive an age-old discussion over means and ends.

Technology, however sophisticated and inspiring to the imagination of technologists, will not automatically result in the benefits that are sometimes forecast by its advocates. The history of technology shows a disappointing repetition of instances of predicted revolutions that subsequently failed to materialize. In the majority of these cases of stunted growth, the attention to the means overshadowed the concern with the ends. The pursuit of ever more hi-tech forms of technology and increased access to technology can only be justified by our expectations about their potential contribution to a better world. Just chasing after the hottest technologies is a shallow pursuit and not worth the excitement it often generates.

The overriding questions are: What are our goals, how do these goals relate to creating a better world, and how do the technologies we pursue help achieve our goals? In the domain of education, a greater level of complexity surrounds these questions. Not only are the emerging technologies affecting the means by which we facilitate learning, they are also influencing the ends themselves. As they both provoke and facilitate the shift from an "industrial" model of society to a post-industrial information society , they are, in fact, implicitly re-defining the fundamental nature of learning and teaching.

There is an intimate link between developments in the world of learning and those that pertain to the information society. This relationship will be analyzed in more detail in the sections that follow. The learning side of the equation will be tackled first. Two perspectives will particularly be highlighted: the recognition that learning is an innate ingredient of our very humanity and the ensuing concern that conventional learning environments are not well-suited for meeting society's learning objectives. We live in a time that learning is taking on a distinctly enhanced meaning. It is a time when changes in the learning environment, which have been advocated for decades if not centuries, are becoming necessary rather than merely desirable.

Learning is an essential basis for both action and reflection and thus for creativity and problem solving. Learning is a pursuit in its own right which goes beyond the utilitarian conceptions that have for a long time related it almost exclusively to the world of work. In developing and industrialized nations alike, change, and consequently the need to respond and adapt to change and to manage ensuing conflict, are fundamental ingredients of life. Learning is the mechanism through which human beings cope with — and in turn contribute to — change. The possibility to engage in learning throughout one's life and across multiple dimensions of life is thus essential for survival as well as a condition for continual quality of life.

The traditional perceptions regarding education, based on the assumption that learning is the prerogative of the young, and that adult learning is at worst a response to failure and at best a marginal supplement, an exception rather than the rule, are becoming rapidly outdated. Learning is increasingly seen as a lifelong and life-wide requirement. This is contrary to the notion of learning as a mere preparation for life — with a discrete beginning and end — but not as an integral part of life.

To be a productive and participating member of society, one needs to be able to continue to learn, to grow with changes in the environment and to respond to the availability of different opportunities. For example, the increasing emphasis on informal sector activities as well as changing patterns of employment cause linear career paths to be replaced by career networks in which people find themselves exploring distinct environments and moving into divergent directions at various stages of their lives.

Inherent in the emergence of the information society is also the need to rethink the priorities accorded to work-related activities vis-à-vis activities not directly related to the world of work. This is particularly relevant considering that in many societies people now spend decreasing proportions of their active life on what traditionally would be called 'work' and increased proportions of it on activities that would traditionally have been seen as pertaining to 'leisure.' Quality of life, then, becomes less a function of self-realization in the (formal and informal) work environment and more a dimension of, for instance, social, cultural and political participation in society. The boundaries between work, leisure and learning start gradually to disappear and learning becomes a dimension of a work/learning/leisure merger. Learning for work, learning for leisure, and learning for learning are all valid options within that context.

The above conceptualization requires us to rethink traditional learning goals, such as literacy. Literacy has long been seen as a gateway to the world of learning. However, its definition as the ability to describe and interpret the world in terms of alphanumeric symbols is no longer adequate. There are many literacies and, consequently, illiteracies.

Technological illiteracy, political illiteracy, ecological illiteracy, intercultural illiteracy, and so many other ways in which people are hindered in their ability to act and reflect upon their environment are just as important as the inability to read and write. Across these various literacies there is a growing problem of information overload which threatens to paralyze us. The inability to process and critically analyze information is increasingly a concern. Learners must develop the ability to access and process huge volumes of information so as to create meaning and generate new knowledge.

The world has known unmet learning needs as long as education has been a conscious concern of societies. What is new now is that such unmet learning needs can no longer be seen as isolated phenomena within the boundaries of particular countries or distinct parts of the world. The world is increasingly becoming a global society and a learning place in its own right. The extent to which the world will be able to learn, will condition its survival and its ability to make the planet an acceptable, and hopefully desirable, place to live.

Global learning depends on the ability of societies to turn themselves into learning societies and of communities within societies to constitute themselves as learning communities. In turn, learning communities exist to the extent that their individual members are learning individuals. But what is the global reality? As we approach the end of the second millennium, there are still more than 900 million illiterate people in the world. New illiterates emerge every day as the result of inadequate school systems, inappropriate curricula, and insufficient conditions to prevent relapse into illiteracy once people have become literate .

More than 130 million school-age children worldwide do not go to school. The millions that do go to school often fall victim to the diploma disease, ending up with learning achievements that do not relevantly relate to their immediate needs nor guarantee that learning sustains throughout their lives. School systems, as we know them, reflect the requirements of the formal economy and, besides their obvious role in serving the learning needs of new generations, they also serve as channels for the socialization of human beings into the pre-existing socio-economic hierarchies pertaining to the formal system. They are ill-equipped to respond to the learning challenges and opportunities of the future.

Schools are burdended with a great deal of pressure due to increasing demand. In the past, they served a smaller and less diverse clientele, often already in many ways pre-selected. Today's schools are expected to carry out the almost impossible task of meeting the diverse needs of many more students. In its advice to UNESCO's Executive Board, the 'Ad Hoc Forum of Reflection on UNESCO's Role in the Last Decade of the Twentieth Century' concluded in 1993 that "education is increasingly necessary and less and less possible, due to its cost."

Furthermore, many schools are weakened by outdated structures which constitute an impediment to learning. Among these barriers are the continued reliance on the artificial separations between levels of education, such as primary, secondary and tertiary, or between socio-economically biased different tracks of learning, such as academic and vocational or technical. Equally inappropriate are often the ways in which human knowledge has become compartmentalized in stale curricula and presented in ways that are relevant, if at all, only for portions of society. Furthermore, these curricula tend to narrowly concentrate only on a small portion of the intelligence spectrum. During the 1980's various researchers reviewed and broadened the concept of intelligence.

Mainstream schools sometimes have difficulty in acknowledging other learning environments, other partners, or other systems of knowledge. They are furthermore limited — and are at great risk to rapidly grow almost totally out of touch with developments in society at large in often continuing to rely heavily on teachers as the main source of knowledge and information. With the changes taking place in society, schools are in dire need to de-formalize and re-constitute themselves as components of learning environments that facilitate people's mobility across a wide range of options to participate in society at large as well as in their local communities.

The world is changing at a scale and pace and with a level of interdependency to which we are previously unaccustomed. This phenomenon of hyperchange is a combination of linear, exponential, discontinuous and chaotic change. Several forces, including the proliferation of information and communication technologies, the rapid production and flows of information, the globalization of fragile financial markets coupled with the parallel growth of informal local economies, the decentralization of governments and bureaucracies, the intense marketing of certain cultural fantasies and lifestyle preferences, and the rise of new political actors, are contributing to the intensifying, complexifying and churning of these change processes.

The current global environment is filled with a great deal of tension, frustration and conflict that is closely linked both to real and perceived shifts in power, glaring inadequacies of 'modern' institutions that are being continually revealed, and a nagging uncomfortability which is tied to the inherent unpredictability and uncontrollability surrounding hyperchange. The vision of a rational world order so eloquently articulated by the architects of the 20th century i.e., scientists, economists, and WWII statesmen, is becoming increasingly questioned in terms of both its achievability and desirability. Over the past three hundred years, the paradigm of modernity has played a significant role in shaping dominant notions of development, progress, growth, freedom, democracy, and social justice.

However, several sacred intellectual spaces that have been closely linked to modernity are currently being contested and renegotiated on various terrains and at various levels of our day-to-day lives. These challenged spaces include: the mechanistic/ reductionist views of systems vs. complexity, the objective vs. the subjective, the modern vs. the traditional, the universal vs. the culturally specific and pluralistic, the public vs. the private, the real vs. the virtual, the secular vs. the religious, the urban vs. the rural, individual vs. the community, the male vs. female vs. gender, the nation-state vs. the supra-national vs. local, and the individual vs. community.

Such contestations, on one hand, provide several reasons for optimism by opening up opportunities for shifting power and resources, generating new discourses and language, remapping borders, creating new identities, and liberating relationships. They also at the same, however, place tremendous pressure on the paradigm of modernity which can be expected to result in a multitude of skirmishes, shocks, bumps, dislocations, breaks, and ruptures as we try to come to grips with a messy world.

The levels of violence and destruction underlying these will no doubt be influenced by the global threats of militarization (further enhanced through increasing decentralization and commercialization of weapons), environmental degradation, and socio-psychological alienation. What should be viewed as particularly worrisome though is that the phenomenon of hyperchange places a severe strain on our present abilities to make sense of, contextualize, adapt to, negotiate, and influence the opportunities and conflicts taking place around us.

Many societies lack both relevant shared narratives and a respect for and understanding of other peoples' narratives. Many individuals and communities around the world today lack the ability to generate, link (the past, present and future), and evolve multiply interconnected personal narratives which provide them with a sense of meaning beyond themselves. The ability to generate new meanings in socially constructive, pluralistic and non-violent ways can be seen to be constrained, to a large degree, by a breakdown of several social self-referencing mechanisms and feedback processes.

We are confronted with a seemingly paralyzing inability to introduce, interact around and utilize new ideas. Anti-intellectual approaches masked under the rhetoric for 'pragmatism', 'practicality', 'implementation', and under false dichotomies of academic vs. practitioner and theory vs. action, are dramatically reducing the spaces for engaging in more critical, constructive and participatory forms of intellectual discourse which are essential for reflecting upon and challenging the ideological basis of how societies are being forced to conceive of their development.

The results are the we are unable to generate new visions to give context to our ideas and new ideas to give greater context to our visions. In addition, dominant analytical frameworks, methodologies, discourse, and interactions are not robust and dynamic enough to help us understand and respond in creative and diverse ways to the complex challenges that face the world. Yet, we continue to attempt to construct mechanistic, first-order, single-discipline solutions to address these. Furthermore, most 'educated' people have been socialized to only see narrow immediate realities and isolated contexts which tend to be mired in the logic of functionalism, economic efficiency, cost-effectiveness, and risk averseness. Their ideas and positions are reduced to specific places, fixed periods of times, and rigid definitions of identity and social roles such as low caste, women, minority, left/ right, etc.

We are also faced with a breakdown in our 'institutions of reflection' i.e., the multiple socio-spiritual spaces in which we engage in ethical self-reflection, sense-making, and dialogue about our attitudes and priorities and their links to our behavior and actions. Such institutions are critical to enhancing our awareness and consciousness, to continuously rejuvenating our optimism and hope, and to supporting our engagement in a process of radical transformation. However, having been simultaneously attacked by both the nihilistic forces of liberalism/post-modernism and preserved/handcuffed by the forces of conservatism , these spaces are either disappearing or becoming antequated and irrelevant. Many of our surviving and emerging institutions prevent us from having the time to think about the different changes taking place around us and our relationship to these. They also allow for dangerous levels of anonymity for the participants which has serious consequences for notions of social responsibility.

Conventional notions of leadership have typically been framed in terms of those people who are in the elite ranks of governments, business, other organizations, rather than, in terms of all of us being leaders in different facets of our lives. This has created a situation in which individuals are easily allowed to defer their personal responsibility for actions to the 'other.' Many practiced models of leadership are still grounded in notions of authoritarianism and hoarding of power with the guiding metaphors of self-preservation and manipulation. Many of our leaders have tended to adopt and hide behind positions based on the real-politik, partisanism and cynicism, and lack the courage and confidence to take bold risks in new directions. Preferring to preach dogma, they lack the ability to inspire others to create meaning in their lives.

The crisis of meaning can be seen as being linked to the failures of modern education systems, and, more broadly, to limitations and biases of the dominant paradigm of development. Our responses to this complex crisis have thus far disappointingly consisted of models that assume simplistic linear causalities which, on one level, have led to calls for more schools, formalized non-formal centers, and distance education modalities; and, on another level, have invoked and glorified a fool's paradise based on ever-increasing levels of economic growth/consumption and technological innovation. These responses, for the most part, have lacked a deeper understanding of and commitment to supporting the processes of change that are required to radically transform systems. They have been narrowly framed in terms of advancing the agenda of the economic and material rather than in terms of a more profound struggle to discover what it means to be 'fully human.'

The dialectical lifelong processes of discovery and self-realization, both on individual and collective levels, should serve to guide a much broader philosophy of learning which extends far beyond the conventional classroom and one-dimensional standardized tests.

The responses to the crisis of meaning by the international development community have thus far centered around schooling with increasing calls for more 'basic education,' 'functional literacy,' and 'skills training' opportunities. Several generalizations can be made concerning how the institution of schooling has been developed and, in many cases, continues to be reproduced around the world:

1. Schools have been shaped by ideological and philosophical traditions of development which are increasingly being challenged. The inter-connected logics of colonialism (civil servants, conversion and racial superiority), industrialization and human capital theory (workers, managers and jobs), modernization (modern/Western outlooks, in direct opposition to traditional), nation-building (national identity and allegiance to the state) and globalization (consumerism and competition) have played

significant roles, at different points in history, in shaping the values, goals, structure, timing, processes, and activities of schools. Schooling is predominantly driven by the development imperatives of the state. Thus, the rationale guiding schools has been strongly biased towards supporting the urbanized formal sectors of government and large scale industry. Schooling has served to 'mainstream' and socialize people into fitting into the dominant culture with the focus on maintenance learning. "The acquisition of fixed outlooks, methods and rules for dealing with known and recurring situations. It enhances our problem-solving ability for problems that are given. It is the type of learning designed to maintain an existing system or an established way of life". There is virtually no ideological space provided for challenging existing knowledge frameworks and constructing alternative ways of seeing, believing, and doing.

2. "Three mechanistic metaphors have historically contextualized our view of schooling and learning: the universe as a clock, the brain as a computer, and learning as tabula rasa (blank slate)". Assumptions derived from these metaphors, and further elaborated through theories of Skinnerian behavioralism, Piagetian developmental psychology and Darwinistic individualism, still underlie dominant structure and practice in conventional education systems. Schools and the processes of teaching and learning are predicated on the institutional desire to instill control and discipline. The effect, as Papert describes, is that "the institution of School, with its daily lesson plans, fixed curriculum, standardized tests, and other such

paraphernalia, tends constantly to reduce learning to a series of technical acts and the teacher to the role of a technician."

3. Education systems have tended to be conceived of as rigid and isolated entities. Schools have been developed as compartmentalized, closed systems that are delinked from their external communities. Learning in schools is seen as separate from and unconnected to the learning that takes place in non-formal and informal environments. Most schools have refused to acknowledge that learners spend more time in the informal environment than they do in schools. The validity of other spaces for learning, other knowledge systems, and other partners in the learning/teaching process has often been neglected, and even, devalued. Furthermore, there has been very little flexibility within the system. It has been organized along strict linear levels of education i.e, the 'stages' approach, with artificial separations such as primary, secondary and tertiary. Schooling takes place within inflexible blocks of time which require learners to be present on a year-long basis.

4. Parents and students' objectives for engaging in schooling have been narrowly centered around obtaining a job with the primary focus on doing well on the examination and obtaining a certificate. In this setting, there has been little value attributed to learning as an essential process in the wider context of life. Schooling has been conceived of as taking place only in the early years in one's life, and learning is thought to be completed when one graduates and receives a diploma i.e., signifying that one is 'educated.' Furthermore, the exam-orientation has tended to lead towards approaches tied to

memorizing a large repertoire of facts and routines with little concern over whether the learner actually understands and can apply different information and skills in constructive ways. Learning has become a ritual. Schools have, for the most part, failed to establish a culture of learning that extends beyond the walls of the classroom.

5. Schooling has been primarily framed in terms of knowledge and value transmission. Gardner describes that, "In the outmoded view of learning that dominates our institutions, knowledge is regarded as an objective substance that can be deposited directly into people's minds. Education is seen as the process by which knowledge is transferred into the learner's minds, and teaching is seen as the packaging of knowledge for efficient transfer." The focus has been on teaching rather than supporting learning and understanding. Learners have been regarded as 'empty vessels' and the range of knowledge and cultural experiences that they already come to school with is hardly acknowledged.

6. There is very little sensitivity to the diversity of learners. The system has been constructed along the lines of factory in the tradition of Fordism. Within this framework, learning interventions have been typically designed for the imaginary "mean" learner. There is very little flexibility for catering to the specific differences of learners -- their individual personalities, culture, linguistic, learning styles, family background, motivational levels, interests and special needs. Furthermore, the system fails to take into account the physical, emotional, social and cognitive abilities of each learner. However, Gardner

describes, "What science about learning tells us is that human abilities are diverse in their form range and development and are intensely individual--they do not match the mass production standards of schooling."

7. Many educators mistakenly believe that intelligence is a static, unmodifiable trait, and that potential and capability are finite. "The IQ way of thinking says that people are either smart or not, are born that way, that there's nothing you can do about it, and that tests can tell you if you are one of the smart ones or not". Under this scenario, the 'smart' students enter into a virtuous cycle of praise, support and achievement, while those deemed as 'dumb' enter into a vicious cycle of self-doubt, neglect and failure. Closely linked to this notion, is a general fallacy that success in learning depends more on pure ability than on effort.

8. Curricula have been framed in tightly compartmentalized and fragmented disciplines, with content and materials that tends to be irrelevant to most learners, often favoring a strong urban and middle-class bias. Gardner adds that, "Indeed, as currently constituted, our educational system is heavily biased towards linguistic modes of instruction and assessment and, to a somewhat lesser degree, towards logical quantitative modes as well." Several critiques have also been raised about the propensity of schooling to alienate individuals from their rural, ethnic and linguistic communities. The focus of curricula has been on developing abstract, academic, and generalized learning, with little attention to contextualized, reflective, emotional learning.

9. Curricula have been conceptualized with the understanding that learning takes place in chunked, linear stages starting with notions like 'functional literacy' and 'basic education' constituting the first stage with later stages focusing on higher order levels of thinking. Lauren Resnick refutes this conceptualization, arguing that so-called "higher order thinking isn't higher order. Higher order thinking refers to reasoning, arguments, problem-solving, and so on. Thinking should not be seen as some esoteric add-on. The most basic and seemingly elementary performances require active strategic thinking."

9. Learning in the classroom has been seen as a predominantly individualistic activity. Competition has been viewed as a far more powerful motivator than cooperation. Sharing with, assisting and collaborating with fellow learners on projects is typically called 'cheating' and is punished. Fear and mistrust (of students and teachers) have shaped most schooling models. To support this, there is a strong hierarchy built into the school.

10. The learner is seen to be subordinate to the teacher, who is viewed as the omnipotent expert, with classroom roles largely fixed. In turn, the teacher is subordinate to the principal and inspectors. The learner, the teacher, and communities have very little opportunity to participate in the identification of learning goals and the development of curriculum. The processes by which learners learn from other learners, their parents and communities, and in other environments are also not encouraged. Furthermore, by isolating learners into age groups,

schooling has not fostered activities that would involve both adults and children learning together and geared towards building greater understanding between them.

11. The liberal democratic tradition has argued that 'schooling for all' serves as a mechanism for the creation of a democratic and egalitarian society. Schooling is supposed to be a great equalizing and empowering force. However, schooling and its claims towards producing meritocracy has been strongly critiqued on the grounds that it reproduces hierarchical socio-economic relations and reinforces existing notions around the distribution of power. Many countries today, for example, still have education systems that feature different socio-economically biased tracks of learning, such as academic and vocational/ technical, which tend to lead to different predetermined roles, opportunities and power in society. Illich has also described the feelings of 'psychological impotence' i.e., the inability of people to fend for themselves, that are cultivated in students in relation to the dominant socio-economic institutions. Those who drop-out or are forced out of the system are labeled failures and leave feeling humiliated, bitter, frustrated, and demoralized. Naik has analyzed this process at work in India which is equally applicable to many countries of the South, "The main achievement of the system, therefore, is to condemn the bulk of children of common people as dropouts and failures and to consign them to a life of drudgery and poverty which has hardly any parallel in the contemporary world or even in our own earlier history." Worse yet, these human beings leave the system believing that their failure is solely their fault.

These critiques are by no means exhaustive and serve to highlight only certain concerns about the limitations of schooling. The extent to which this alphabet of generalizations applies to any particular context can, of course, be extensively debated. Positive examples can be found in the education system, but these occur in spite of the system rather than because of it. What should emerge from this discussion is that most educational systems today still remain insensitive to the widely diverse needs of learners of all age groups and ignorant to the complexity of learning processes. Furthermore, the institutionalized intervention of schooling has provided little space and empowerment for both individual learners and learner groups to engage in the construction of alternative visions of development. Marshall describes that, "By design, we constructed and operated our Newtonian schools as we understood this world, and this produced iatrogenic and learning-disabled institutions that have suppressed reflective thought, creativity, and the innate and inexhaustible human capacity for lifelong growth." Such critique extends far beyond the school as being elitist, classist, racist or sexist. It raises fundamental questions around the school as being a dehumanizing and socially destructive force in society.

What must be viewed as particularly disturbing, however, as we look towards the future, is our continued obsession with the institution of 'schooling' as the central reference point for learning; the increasing demands we place on it as a panacea for solving society's problems; and our inability to 'see' and stimulate other dynamic learning spaces. For example, many current efforts by the international development community as part of the Education for All movement are primarily geared towards extending the system "to the unreached" by expanding existing delivery mechanisms and improving the management and financing of these.

Distance education, commonly defined as Aan educational process in which a significant proportion of the teaching is conducted by someone removed in space and time from the learner, is gaining immense popularity among these modalities. While distance education serves to provide an added element of flexibility, most efforts (as they are predominantly motivated by cost considerations) do not address the deeper problems that confront education systems as they have tended to be conceived of as extensions of the school. Such activities fail to confront the ideological contradictions and systemic conservativeness of schooling.

Formal schooling, whether in person or at a distance, is an inappropriate solution by itself for dealing with the development challenges and opportunities of the future. Fullan , after extensive review of change initiatives, argues that introducing new innovations and reforms into current educational systems is "an ultimately fruitless uphill battle" as these systems have been designed to be resistant to change. He calls for "a new mindset about educational change."

Thinking and acting in terms of open learning communities signifies a concerted effort to resituate our means and ends in both education and in development -- from a model of learning for development to learning is development. It represents an attempt to put into use and practice much of what we already know. The term 'open learning communities' is presented here in order to deliberately challenge the reader to think of learning beyond the conventional school-teacher-textbook modalities -- to facilitate a shift from a culture of schooling to a culture of learning. The term should be seen as a symbolic descriptor representing the dynamic convergence of several ideological vectors (comprised of theories, movements, mini-revolutions, acts of resistance, and feelings of hope that are carriers of change) from around the world. What this convergence provides is a set of principles, experiences and commitments that not only serve to challenge some of the basic assumptions and goals around how education systems have been conceptualized and implemented in the modern world, but also start to form a legitimized space for constructing new alternatives. The convergence brings a generative dimension to it whereby the effect of each ideological vector is increased by its simultaneous contribution to increasing the power of other vectors.

Concept of open learning communities

The concept of open learning communities is motivated by three sets of inter-connected goals:

> To assist individuals in engaging in diverse processes and contexts which allow them to develop their full human potential -- as individual persons, as family members, as member of different communities, as part of humanity as well as at a spiritual level. This requires us to recognize the diversity of both individuals and communities, their particular needs and aspirations, and the different roles and capacities which people are required to play in diverse cultural settings. It also requires us to recognize that learning also takes place at an organizational level.

- To assist each individual and community in participating in meaningful ways to the decisionmaking and management functions of society. This implies that people must be empowered to access various participation opportunities as well as to contribute to the creation of new participation opportunities.14 They must continually learn to play new roles in different settings. They must be empowered to read the world with various relational lenses.
- To assist individuals and communities in engaging in the processes of creatively, responsibly and non-violently constructing alternative paradigms for development that are consistent with the ideals of mutual respect, compassion, trust, fairness and sacrifice. Such alternative paradigms should envision the renewal of human relationships and the rebuilding of families and communities, the transformation of institutions, the fundamental redistribution of resources and reconceptualization of power along more equitable and sustainable (grounded in conservation) lines, and the creation of respect for all forms of life and our natural environment.

At the outset that there is no such thing as a simple, replicable "open learning community" that provides all things to all learners (although this may appear to be an obvious statement, it actually represents quite a profound shift from the way in which we have attempted to develop education systems -- as one-stop shopping -- over the past 50 years). Rather, there should exist a multiplicity of diverse, layered, interconnected open learning communities.

Each particular open learning community can be seen to evolve out of specific cultural and historical processes, out of a response to a specific set of local/ global problems, and out of dynamic interactions with its environment, other open learning communities and the contributions of the individuals who choose to participate in it. While there is no one pre-defined or pre-fabricated model of an open learning community, we can, however, begin to articulate some principles (that are not fixed, but evolving) which contribute to envisioning open learning communities.

To better explain the concept, the phrase will first be taken apart in order to lay out some of the key dimensions and implications of the terms "open", "learning", and "community." Although this approach may appear to be a bit artificial or fragmentary, transforming the world of learning requires us to question and rethink the basic underpinnings of how we see the world in terms of problems and opportunities, how we engage in processes of learning, and how we interact with each other. The phrase will then be re-assembled and discussed as a dynamic whole.

As has been indicated, the vision of open learning communities is continually growing and evolving. The following exercise should therefore be viewed as an initial attempt to illustrate some key ideological vectors that are driving the notion of open learning communities rather than provide a precise comprehensive definition (which ultimately might prove to be counter-productive and restrictive). Others, of course, will have differing interpretations about the concept of open learning communities. It is therefore important that we encourage such differences while at the same time, engaging in processes of dialogue centered around further elaborating, clarifying, sharing and reconfiguring certain understandings and frames of reference.

The use of the term 'open' is strongly linked to processes of opening up the ways in which we see and understand the world. Capra describes that "the more we study the major problems of our time, the more we come to realize that they cannot be understood in isolation." The concept of open is thus grounded in systems thinking -- a discipline for seeing wholes. Frameworks and approaches linked to the term open seek to liberate us from mechanistic approaches, reductionist thinking, rigid hierarchical structures, linear processes, isolated modalities, and bivalent thinking (i.e., two-valuedness, two ways to answer each question, true or false, 1 or 0). Several dimensions of the term 'open' merit further elaboration:

Open can be used to describe dynamic systems and the interplay between them. All things that evolve in the real world, be they physical, chemical, biological, ecological, or even social systems, are dynamic open entities that continually interchange energy, matter and information with their environment to stay alive. The boundaries are seen as semi-permeable rather than absolute. Flows occur horizontally among units as well as vertically between different layers. Open systems are thus vulnerable to change within their own structures and also have the potential to change other systems.

Open thinking involves being able to see underlying structures and inter-relationships rather than linear cause-effect chains. It is closely linked to the notion of deep ecology which "sees the world not as a collection of isolated objects, but as a network of phenomena that are fundamentally interconnected and interdependent. Deep ecology (as distinguished from shallow ecology which is anthropocentric) recognizes the intrinsic value of all living beings and views humans as just one particular strand in the web of life". Within this context, there is a change in emphasis from viewing entities and organizational relationships in terms of hierarchical modes towards promoting more heterarchical linkages, i.e., systems in which each element is equally ruled by others.

Open thinking involves the ability to shift analyses and reference points back and forth between different levels of systems (non-hierarchical systems nested within other systems) and across systems. It involves being able to move between different contexts and across different disciplines of knowledge. It also entails being able to connect different contexts and disciplines into more holistic frameworks. Open thinking involves seeing change in terms of processes rather than as isolated snapshots. Such processes often take place in dynamic non-linear and unpredictable ways. This implies that we be willing to view conceptions of time differently. Time is conventionally perceived as being monochromatic in which events and acts follow in a certain definite sequence. Polychronic conceptions of time are used to describe different phenomena occurring simultaneously. Time is not understood in a linear way but rather as a set of certain points of mutual reference. Herman describes that, "Polychronic notions of time to a much larger degree admit the possibility of jump (qualitative) changes."

Open thinking involves fuzziness—seeing the world in infinite shades of gray between black and white, not only in black in white terms. The fuzzy principle states that everything is a matter of degree. Fuzziness means multivalence i.e., three or more options, perhaps an infinite spectrum of options, instead of just two extremes. It is about living with contradictions: moving from a world of 'A OR not-A' to considering that 'A AND not-A' can both exist. Artificial divisions of formal, non-formal and informal education have little relevance as categories in isolation of each other. It calls for us to recognize that we all live in "mediatized environments where education is simply one of many different cultural experiences". It asks that we think in multichannel terms -- designing approaches based on our understanding of the multiple channels that support different types learning processes and that learners engage in within a particular environment. This also involves discovering new ways to link these individual channels together. Within this context, it is important to understand how information flows between channels and environments and seek to stimulate different flows of information.

Open thinking also questions the value of using nation-states and geo-political borders as the primary unit of analyses for discussing learning systems. It pushes us to see institutions and policies in terms of horizontally and vertically overlapping layers ranging from the local to global. In addition, the idea of open calls for the introduction of more flexibility by moving away from constrictive and debilitating linear levels/ grades, divisions of education, and rigid time frames.

The notion of open questions the value of using bivalent categories to describe complex realities such as: educated and uneducated, literate and illiterate, enrolled and unenrolled, developed and developing, rich and poor, modern and traditional, and so on. It pushes us to think beyond using isolated categories of race, class, gender. It strongly challenges the use of development strategies that target specific groups in isolation of each other such as out-of school and unemployed youth, drop-outs, street children, marginalized women, the poorest of the poor, unreached, etc. Escobar problematizes the use of single labels to describe human beings and social relationships, "The use of labels such as 'small farmer' or 'pregnant women' reduces a person's life to a single trait and makes him/her a case to be treated or transformed. The use of labels also allows experts and elites to delink explanations of 'the problem' from themselves as the non-poor, and assign them purely to factors internal to the poor."

Open also encourages us to think more holistically and moves away from highly compartmentalized and isolated disciplinary approaches towards more integrated frameworks. It encourages the building of linkages across sectors, for example, between learning, health, culture, politics and economics. It also requires that we acknowledge the validity of other knowledge systems. There is a heterarchical space for a plurality of voices. Finally, the idea of open challenges us to look at our work in development and education in terms of dynamic, continuous processes rather than as discrete projects which will result in easily definable end-products. The international development community must come to recognize that the future can neither be predicted nor manufactured.

The notion of 'learning' is a very broad and multi-dimensional one. Learning has implications for how people search for, acquire, analyze, synthesize, use and share information and skills from a variety of media; how they perceive themselves, reflect on their condition and negotiate their identities; how they connect with others and their environments; how they seek to express themselves, grow, and develop their own capacities to continue to learn; and how they construct meaning and evolve their consciousness. Because of its inherent "ephemeralness and unpredictability" and the diversity of contexts in and purposes for which it takes place, learning is extremely difficult to describe. Rather than attempt to provide an extensive overview of learning, this part will merely serve to highlight a few aspects of learning that are particularly relevant to the concept of open learning communities.

There is a wide range of goals that exist for learning which are culturally, systemically and learner defined. A few goals which incorporate both individual and societal dimensions for why we learn are discussed. We learn both for survival and in order to give greater meaning to our lives. The Delors Commission suggests the following broad set of goals: Learning to Know, Learning to Do, Learning to Live Together, Learning to Be. Imbedded in these is a long-term dimension of learning as well as a perspective that cuts across all domains of life i.e., the goals of learning are not limited to only succeeding in the economic or formal sectors.

These goals are also not seen as static and are given meaning through the interpretations of different communities and individuals which allows them to go beyond being words on a piece of paper. Within this context, there is an understanding that spaces must be provided for interacting around the goals of learning in a pluralistic and participatory manner, in which there is strong respect and value given to different belief systems, knowledge systems, cultural values, and languages. We can also see the goals of learning in terms of processes which provide for the varying cognitive, emotional, psycho-social, health and nutritional, moral/ethnical, cultural/artistic, technological, participation, ecological and spiritual needs of individuals and communities.

Within the framework of open learning communities, there is a conscious attempt to link understandings and lessons from the past and the present towards actively constructing the future. This implies creating contexts in which we are expected to make mistakes and in which we are encouraged to learn from our mistakes. This also involves a shift in emphasis from status quo-based approaches which have supported maintenance learning. Rather, there should be a concerted effort to promote innovative learning which prepares individuals and communities to deal with "new situations through the integration, synthesis, and the broadening of horizons. Its meaning derives from dissonance among contexts. It leads to critical questioning of conventional assumptions behind traditional thoughts and actions, focussing on necessary changes. Innovative learning advances our thinking by reconstructing wholes, not by fragmenting reality". Underlying the idea of innovative learning is the belief that learning involves interacting, meaning-making, reflecting and creating.

In the context of open learning communities, learning is conceived of as a continuous, asynchronous lifelong process that individuals and communities engage in through a variety of experiences and interactions. "Lifelong learning no longer refers simply to recurrent education or to a second chance for those who missed out in the first instance. Rather, it is a genuine lifelong endeavor, from the cradle to the grave.". The notion of learning challenges popular thinking which believes that learning is the prerogative and responsibility of the young. It argues that one is never too old to learn. Active learning can and does take place at all ages. The brain is remarkably plastic, constantly learning throughout the span of one's life.

The notion of learning to learn is essential if individuals and communities are to actively engage in the processes of discovering and creating the 'for what?' of learning. Advances in neuroscience tell us that there is no limit to growth and to the capacities of humans to learn more. Neurons continue to be capable of making new connections throughout life. Every human being can learn to be more intelligent. There are no longer categories of 'smart' and 'dumb' learners. All people can learn to become more effective, flexible and organized learners. What becomes important in this context is our ability to continually develop the capacities to tap into our potential. "The deeper meaning of learning to learn is associated with learners learning to extend and master their own capacities for learning". Learning to learn also calls for extending the notion of literacy beyond its functional definition to include multicultural literacy, technological literacy, democratic literacy, ecological literacy, critical media literacy, and so on.

Each person develops a concept of 'self-as-learner.' Learning to learn involves developing oneself: to engage in critical reflection and creative thinking; to open up to other people's ideas, attitudes, and feelings; to become aware of and access learning resources through a variety of media; to recognize and question one's implicit assumptions; and to become less fearful of change. Learning to learn is also closely associated with processes that encourage us to think about our learning. Metacognition is used to refer to an awareness of thought processes, and metamood is an awareness of one's own emotions. The term self-awareness reflects an ongoing attention to one's internal states. The capacity for self-awareness is directly linked to individuals becoming self-directed learners, taking responsibility for their own learning.

Though we all have the same set of physical systems, we must begin to recognize and appreciate the diverse, complex, multifaceted nature of each human learner. Some of this difference is a consequence of our genetic endowment. Some of it is a consequence of differing experiences and differing environments. The diversity is expressed in terms of personality and interests, cultures and family background, differing talents and intelligences, learning styles, motivation levels, and special needs. Vast ranges in diversity are characterize what it means to be fully human. Several theories related to intelligence have emerged, for example, to support the notion of diverse learners and learning processes. Gardner has advanced the idea that there are at least seven different human intelligences that allow us to engage in learning in order to make sense of the world:

(1) language;

(2) logical-mathematical analysis;

(3) spatial representation;

(4) musical thinking;

(5) the use of the body to solve problems or to make things;

(6) an understanding of other individuals; and,

(7) an understanding of ourselves.

Robert Sternberg has put forth categories of componential intelligence, creative intelligence and practical intelligence. Perkins offers the neural, reflective, and experiential aspects of intelligence. Goleman raises the dimension of emotional intelligence which includes: "abilities such as being able to motivate oneself and persist in the face of frustrations; to control impulse and delay gratification; to regulate one's moods and keep distress from swamping the ability to think; to empathize and to hope." Every human being has his or her own complex portfolio of intelligences. Learners' abilities to engage in learning are derived from these different intelligences which are called upon in different contexts. It should be clarified that the idea of a portfolio of intelligences is not fixed. Learning also involves processes for allowing us to continually develop, connect and enhance our different human intelligences. Learning should thus be viewed as an intensely personal experience.

Students do not learn the same way. Each individual learner has a set of preferred ways of taking in and processing information and expressing themselves as well as their own paces at which they do so. They also have their own preferred learning environments. Learning style researchers, for example, point out that individual differences exist such as the preference for learning alone or in groups, concretely or abstractly, through books, charts, computers, video, oral stories and debates, etc. At the same time, different senses, different mind/brain attributes (such as conscious/ unconscious learning) and different media/channels influence how different learners process information, construct meaning and express themselves.

Different multisensory interactions and modes of communication and expression allow us to see the world in different ways. The challenge that emerges from this understanding of the diversity of learners is the need to both appreciate that learners are different and need choice, while ensuring that they are exposed to a multiplicity of contexts. Underlying this is the critical issue of motivation and support i.e., encouraging learners to take learning risks and assisting them when they 'fail'. Addressing this issue in meaningful ways starts with attempting to value the knowledge, information, experiences, interests, needs, aspirations, and Active Learning Capacity that each individual learner comes to a learning process with. It also involves understanding and validating the sorts of natural learning processes that learners are involved in in various aspects of their lives.

Several other dimensions are important to note when seeking to create learning contexts which nurture learners. Approaches should support situated learning i.e., learning should be placed within a culture of needs and practices that gives the knowledge and skill being learned context, texture and motivation. This involves making concerted efforts to understand, promote and link to the various potential learning channels that learners interact with on a daily basis. In addition, we should to support the creation of "educational settings with thinking-centered learning, where students learn by thinking through what they are learning about" . The processes of learning should be conceptualized as being inherently social. "All learning involves socially organized activity".

Continually learning together is critical to building social relationships, negotiating difference and resolving conflicts. Approaches of collaborative learning and active participation are crucial in this process. Michael Schrage defines collaboration as an act of shared creation and/or shared discovery. In addition, it is important to support different groupings of learners e.g., multi-age, inter-generational, multicultural, cross-gender, cross-class/caste, cross-professions, etc. Within the context of open learning communities, the notion of an omnipotent and omniscient teacher as "expert" is strongly challenged. Classic roles around who is the teacher and who is the learner become mutated and enter into a perpetual state of flux.

Learning is not a value-neutral set of processes. Learning is closely linked to different ideological positions and has political, cultural and socio-economic dimensions. The international development community, however, tends to discuss education as if it were something quite neutral. Very rarely, has this group been required to make explicit its ideological biases. "There neither is, nor has ever been, an educational practice in zero space-time-neutral in the sense of being committed only to preponderantly abstract, intangible ideas". Inherent in the processes of learning is a deeper struggle over discourse and power. "Discourses are not just about what can be said, and thought; but also about who can speak, when, where, and with what authority" (Foucault, 1981). We must therefore continually be aware of the various ideological implications of learning and seek to make explicit our positions and actions within these.

The learning that takes place in schools has been used to reproduce inequities of society or to exclude people from power. Giroux describes that, "What the dominant educational philosophies want is to educate people to adapt to those social forms. Rather than critically interrogate them." In this sense, education follows society. Under a different philosophical orientation, however, learning can be seen as a set of processes to lead society. This is the case if learning is seen as processes of actively constructing knowledge rather than a mechanism for transmitting knowledge. The processes of learning become a means for negotiating identity and (re)defining attitudes, challenging the dominant social order, and reconstructing power, roles and relationships, and reappropriating the social, political, cultural forces that shape the existence of individuals and communities.

The element of 'communities' is critical to consider as it constitutes the socio-cultural context for bringing individuals together to engage in shared meaningful experiences. Such interactions form the basis for learning and for our becoming more fully human. It should be noted that there is no single generic, homogenous, universal community; rather, numerous types of communities exist throughout the world. Although this may seem to be an obvious statement, the international development community's discourse often fails to reflect this understanding as we tend to use the term 'communities' to loosely refer to a widely divergent set of social groupings with different purposes, cultures, scales, etc. Recognizing the complexity and diversity of communities and their associated layers is important to supporting communities.

There are alternative definitions of communities created for a variety of purposes, including those based on:

- geographic affiliations such as a village, rural district or urban areas (it is also important to note that because of modern technologies the community no longer has to be organized only in terms of physical location -- we now witness the emergence of many virtual communities);

- ethnic, racial, linguistic and religious groupings;
- sex and age;
- common occupations, interests, or experiences;
- a resistance to some outside force or threat;
- shared family concerns;
- a general shared philosophy.

Each community has its own peculiar identity which engenders its meaning, purpose, and intentionality and provides coherence around which system stability emerges. Communities are formalized in the sense that they do have some structure, a set of rules and logic to them, and several dimensions of culture. Urevbu describes that, "Specifically, culture consists of language, ideas, beliefs, customs, codes, institutions, tools, techniques, works of art, rituals, ceremonies, and so forth."

Communities also typically have several knowledge systems in parallel operation i.e., oral, public/private, male/female, religious, etc. and they are linked to different social, political, and economic institutions. Communities, however, have different sizes and boundaries. They are open in varying degrees to different types of information and people. Throughout the course of their lives, each individual participates in many different kinds of communities, with varying roles and objectives. A particular community is an evolving space in which the community's own identity and culture and that of its members is continually being defined, challenged, negotiated, and recreated by both its members and by other communities. Communities may emerge, evolve or collapse rather spontaneously through the unplanned interaction of many of dynamic and informal institutions and forces.

There is an intimate link between learning and communities. Strong communities are important for learning, and learning constitutes an important process of building and linking communities. Communities provide a humanizing setting for learning, which has been previously described as an inherently social activity. Communities provide an essential forum for making sense of the world, exploring and building natural historical and cultural ties, negotiating difference, drawing from and building moral and ethical frameworks, and creating development alternatives.

Communities also provide the cultural specificity for situated learning. It is essential, however, that individuals be able to participate in different communities in order to develop different contextual frameworks. It is also important that efforts must be made to mediate and link the learning that takes place in different settings. In the context of open learning communities, a community must be a "safe" space where learners can explore, share and grow. Complex learning is enhanced by challenge and inhibited by threat. The brain/mind learns optimally - it makes maximum connections - when appropriately challenged in an environment which encourages taking risks. Positive emotions such as trust, love, tenderness and humor can facilitate learning. However, the brain/ mind "downshifts" under perceived threat. It then becomes less flexible, and reverts to primitive attitudes and procedures. Negative emotions such as hostility, anger, fear, and anxiety can downshift the brain. This implies that a community must be "personalized" rather than depersonalized i.e., looking at each learner as a special human being that belongs not numbers. Marshall states that within a community, "We must create a learning culture that provides a forum for risk, novelty, experimentation, and challenge."

Learning is also critical to creating new communities and linking them to one another. In recent times, there has been a great deal of romanticization around the notion of traditional communities. In discussing communities, we must not overlook the harsh realities that sometimes exist in many communities such as, resistance to new ideas and problems of unequal power relationships around race, class, gender, sexual preference, caste, age, etc. Nor, should we ignore that communities are often formulated in exclusionary closed terms with membership being tightly controlled. Burnett adds that within communities, "conflict is inevitable and what families and communities learn to do is manage the conflicts to arrive at some measure of agreement, or even to more fully understand what divides them".

Healthy communities are premised on both the individual and organization's ability to enter into dialogue and negotiate conflicts. Learning is the process by which we begin to understand each other, to engage in different roles and relationships, to make sense of the conflicts around us. to see new opportunities for connection and create new identities. Learning is also about strengthening and evolving local knowledge systems and, at the same time, developing self-confidence in one's 'tradition, imagination, intellectual and organizations reserves.' The continued growth of such local knowledge systems coupled with the construction of critical frameworks for viewing other knowledge systems underlie the levels of creativity and sustainability of people-led development movements.

Processes of learning are also critical to connecting communities to each other. As discussed, some communities have been created along more closed boundaries, other communities are sometimes hostile. By bringing in new energy and information and stimulating a process of dialogue, learning can be a force for opening up communities and facilitating meaningful gender-aware, inter-generational, and cross-cultural interactions within a community and across communities.

When put back together, the energy and relationships inherent in open learning communities becomes much greater than simply the sum of its parts. The concept of open learning communities seeks to provide a dynamic alternative framework for seeing and acting in the world. Although I have tried to identify certain principles that are important to the concept, it should be repeated that there is no such thing as one open learning community, nor should there ever be one. Open learning communities represent a celebration of differences and a desire to construct pluralistic environments which promote and foster these differences.

Many examples exist today of the wide range of social groupings that represent potential open learning communities, such as regional configurations, cities and villages; women's associations; youth clubs; workers' cooperatives or unions; corporations and their departments; academic circles; religious groups; extended families; television and radio audiences; and World Wide Web sites. Conventional schools, although currently not considered to operate as open learning communities, can potentially transform themselves into open learning communities.

The principle of self-organization implies the continual spontaneous emergence of diverse new communities and, at the same time, collapse of other communities. Within this context, every open learning community is a learning organism with its own evolving consciousness. Gephart et al. describe "a learning organization is an organization that has an enhanced capacity to learn, adapt and change. It's an organization in which learning processes are analyzed, monitored, developed, managed and aligned with improvement and innovation goals."

Viewed as a complex adaptive system, the open learning community is constantly revising and rearranging its building blocks as it gains experience. It changes and adapt according to the divergent needs and interests of individual learners who participate and contribute to it as well as in response to the broader needs of society. To do this, flexibility, maneuverability and adaptability are important characteristics. This implies that the scale/size of the open learning community becomes critical. Massive systems characterized by rigid hierarchies, rules, structures are ill-equipped to manage change, and even less able to support innovation. In this context, the "small is beautiful" concept takes on a whole new meaning. Systems may be constructed along smaller, more flexible parameters.

An open learning community must also continually reflect on itself in order to remain purposeful. Feedback loops enable a community to regulate itself, correct its mistakes, and re-organize itself. Such feedback loops are integrally linked to a process of being able to listen to voices from within and outside, to learn from them, and to allow the energies inherent in them to facilitate the process of social innovation and transformation. An open learning community is not only capable of adapting or even embracing change, it can generate change from within and can share this change with other open learning communities and their larger environment. In this sense, it is not simply a reactionary entity but rather a pro-active agent of change.

Open learning communities should not be viewed as isolated parts. Rather, they should be seen as a set of relationships operating within a larger learning ecosystem. "The ecosystem concept is defined as a community of organisms and their physical environment interacting as an ecological unit". A learning ecosystem is comprised of a larger physical environment and layers of environments, various open learning communities and their layers, and individual learners who enter into the environment. Within this context, open learning communities, vertically and horizontally layered upon one another (i.e., overlapping), function as networks within networks.

An important aspect of the learning ecosystem is that it optimally uses and distributes the intellectual, experiential, spiritual, and material resources available to it. Lester Brown clarifies that "a sustainable society is one that satisfies its needs without diminishing the prospects of future generations". Another important aspect of the learning ecosystem is biodiversity, both in terms of different forms of life and in terms of cultural and linguistic diversity. Capra describes the essential need for this diversity, "Ethnic and cultural diversity means many different relationships, many different approaches to the same problem. A diverse community is a resilient community, capable of adapting to changing situations." Diversity allows learners and communities to see their problems from varied perspectives and encourages them to develop different ways of dealing with them.

A particular physical environment is comprised of a set of open learning communities which loosely operate within it. However, because of the various layers that exist (i.e., network of networks), a space can simultaneously be both an environment which is comprised of its own associated layers of communities and an open learning community. The institution of UNESCO, for example, is both an open learning community which operates within a larger set of environments, and an environment which supports multiple open learning communities. Each environment has its own architecture and space, information and communication technologies, values, constructs of time, policies and rules, structures, roles, relationships, resources, distribution of power, etc. These are not necessarily the same as those of the open learning communities which they support and sometimes may even contradict them.

The environment plays a large role in influencing the organization and culture of a particular open learning community and its relationship with other open learning communities while, at the same time, the environment is being influenced by the open learning communities. There is a dialectical set of relationships in place. The environment is also critical to supporting the notion of distributed intelligence. Perkins describes this, "The surround-- the immediate physical, social and symbolic15 resources outside the person -- participates in cognition, not just as a source of input and receiver of output but as a vehicle of thought. The surround in a real sense does part of the thinking. . .The surround in a real sense holds part of the learning."

Open learning communities within the same environment also influence and are influenced by each other. The flows of resources, information and energy form the basis for these relationships. Capra describes this sort of interdependence as, "living organisms derive their essential properties and, in fact their very existence from their relationships to other things." Within this context, communities are continuously struggling with the tension of autonomy and differentiation vs. integration. How can an open learning community maintain and evolve its own identity and at the same time be linked to other open learning communities? Power relationships between communities (and cultures) have historically been uneven and exploitative, characterized by Riane Eisler as 'the dominator system of social organization'. These conceptual models need to be replaced with notions of co-evolution (learning and changing together) and partnership. Capra further describes these types of relationships as, "The tendency to associate, establish links, live inside one another, and cooperate." Under such a conceptualization, open learning communities try to complement/ reinforce/ challenge each other to ensure mutual survival rather than dominate one another.

Open learning communities are also influenced by the individuals who choose to participate in them. Land and Hannafin explain, "The learner does not merely respond to the system; rather, he or she is integral to it." Learners are viewed as active constructors of the various open learning communities. Within this framework, individuals are able to participate freely in many different open learning communities, moving in and out as they wish. Notions of membership are loosely defined. In the context of their participation in different learning communities, individuals are given the opportunity to play different leadership roles and engage in different sorts of relationships. These roles and relationships are continually evolving. Open learning communities also serve as institutions of reflection for individuals by continually demanding that people critically reflect on their values, attitudes, feelings, behaviors and actions and by encouraging them to engage in creative dialogue and action.

Despite what the cynics may say, there still does exist multiply diverse spaces for seeing, understanding and interacting in the world and we must continue to support and promote these. Paulo Freire appropriately summarizes the challenge, "We are surrounded by a pragmatic discourse that would have us adapt to the facts of reality. Dream, and utopia, are called not only useless but positively impeding. . . But the attempt to do without hope, in the struggle to improve the world, as if that struggle could be reduced to calculated acts alone, or a purely scientific approach, is a frivolous illusion." Hope is therefore an essential element of open learning communities. The hope which sustains open learning communities is grounded in a belief in the fundamental goodness of human beings and in the beauty of the unpredictability of life.

The concept of open learning communities represents a recognition of the diversity and complexity of learners, learning processes, communities and ways of "seeing" realities. It should be repeated here again that the vision(s) guiding open learning communities is not fixed, nor are the approaches to realizing them. The previous section has attempted to articulate a few elements of what is actually a much more expansive and diverse vision.

The basic thrust of open learning communities lies in utilizing much of what we already know about learning through research and experience, seeing new realities and opportunities, developing new roles and relationships, respecting and fostering diversity, and stimulating new activities in order to give space and life to various socio-spiritual spaces. The implications surrounding the development of open learning communities are, however, immense and overwhelming. They will require that whole new methodologies and frameworks be constructed, new discourses be created, new organizational structures be conceived, new approaches to 'training' be developed, new mechanisms for assessment and evaluation be formulated, and new attitudes be nurtured. Throughout all of this, what will be most important to continually emphasize will be the process of engaging with people around the world to visualize and operationalize their own personal vision and linking this to a complex shared vision(s) of open learning communities.

The process of developing the vision of open learning communities is critical if it is to mean more than words on a piece of paper or slogans of good intention. The process should reflect the idea of ongoing participatory conceptualization i.e., that individuals and communities should not only be responsible for designing, implementing and evaluating open learning communities, but also be integrally involved in a continual process of conceptualizing and modifying the vision that guides them. Each individual and community must seek to understand the ideological and practical implications for themselves and for others, as well as for the present and for the future. Such a process entails a fundamental shift in metaphor -- from that of a book which is written and disseminated by the well-schooled elite to that of an interactive World Wide Web site that is constructed through more participatory and egalitarian methods. The focus of the shift, to clarify, is not on the medium; but rather, on the sets of attitudes, processes and relationships that surround the medium. Botkin et al. describe the traditional metaphor of the book, "The conventional, often unarticulated, conception of how societies learn usually starts with one or more centers of concentrated competence as the emanaters of new discoveries, theories, beliefs and solutions. These new ideas are then disseminated to larger circles of people and the public at large. The role of society at large is reduced to adjusting to and consuming the discoveries and knowledge produced at centers of expertise."

The production of books tends to be linked to elite power structures and centers of concentrated competence. The publishing and distribution channels for books are also tightly controlled. For example, the writing of books is usually done by someone regarded as an 'expert.' Knowledge tends to be seen as fixed and sacred, often regarded as a commodity. With the metaphor of book, the emphasis is on 'dissemination' and 'distribution' whereby readers are typically viewed as passive receivers. The book also, in certain ways, limits our interaction around the ideas that are raised; keeping a safe distance between the writer and the reader.

The structure of the book is typically structured in a linear progression, and must be read in this way. There is very little flexibility for the book to evolve. As we read the book, we can scribble on the margins and underline the words but cannot fundamentally contribute to altering the meaning of the text. Nor, can we engage with the author around the ideas -- the author is allowed to hide behind the medium. We are prevented from entering into constructive dialogue in order to learn from as well as to challenge and influence the author. Out of frustration or anger, individuals may refuse to read books and sometimes try to burn them, but these destructive forms of resistance come with great individual and societal pricetags.

The Internet has been described as a 'great democratizing force'; a liberating and empowering tool. Under the metaphor of the Web site, there is a concerted effort to move from approaches of one-way dissemination to two-way sharing. Such a metaphor is geared around encouraging us to see ourselves as actively constructing and unfolding our own vision of open learning communities, and linking it to the visions of others. Knowledge is seen as dynamic and evolving. The construction of the Web site constitutes a profound shared social experience -- seen as something that the various participants build together. Furthermore, power over the process is transformed. Each one of us can contribute to and modify the vision of the site with text, pictures, sounds, videos; we can interact with each other around ideas; we can hyperlink our sites to other Web sites; we can even create our own sites. We should, however, be very aware that the medium of the Internet is not exempt from attempts at social control -- efforts are currently being made by some institutionally entrenched actors to reproduce the metaphor of the book on the Internet.

Engaging in processes of constructing the open learning community Web sites calls for a special set of attitudes and commitment. It will require that one be willing to move beyond fixing, defending, rationalizing or thinking solely in terms of the institution of schooling. It will mean exploring how to link learning back to the deeper social, political and spiritual problems that face our world. It will require a commitment to enter into the often confusing and frustrating struggle of asking some basic philosophical questions -- who are we as human beings, where are we coming from, and where are we going to. It will involve optimistic risk-taking -- "a willingness to initiate fundamental processes of change, even when all of their implications are not known with total certainty in advance". It will ask that we reconsider our own privileged positions and the power structures to which we derive our authority from. It will require that we be open to experimenting with new ways of sharing and redistributing power.

The obstacles that stand in the way of envisioning open learning communities appear to be quite overwhelming. There are the vested interests of the educational establishment with its teachers' unions and textbook publishers and building contractors. There are the vested interests of the nation-state and resistance of politicians who are unwilling to make decisions which might jeopardize their political power. There are also the vested interests of the development industry which continue to see certain countries and groups as 'developed' and delinked from the problems of the South, and are fundamentally unwilling to challenge this deficit approach. Finally, there is the loosely aligned vested interests of modernity which rely heavily on the institution of schooling to reproduce its ideological frames of reference and socio-economic relationships. These various interest groups threaten to crush the concept of open learning communities.

The world is a dynamic place where new discoveries are continuously being made, new institutions and relationships being formed, new opportunities are emerging. M. Mitchell Waldrop provides some strategic directions, "All complex systems have somehow acquired the ability to bring order and chaos into a special kind of balance. This balance point -- often called the edge of chaos -- is where the components of a system never quite lock into place, and yet never quite dissolve into turbulence, either. The edge of chaos is where new ideas and innovative genotypes are forever nibbling away at the edges of the status quo, and where even the most entrenched old guard will eventually be overthrown."

Our challenge is then to identify and nurture those opportunities at the edges of chaos and to prevent their being co-opted by the various vested interests. The encouraging news is that many positive initiatives are underway throughout the world with new opportunities emerging every day. It is against this mixed backdrop of global and local challenges, intellectual vectors, and obstacles that Learning Without Frontiers is being developed.18 The LWF unit, housed in UNESCO, is attempting to partner with others from around the world who are involved in developing different visions of how to change the world of learning. The LWF unit is also engaged in a perpetual struggle of trying to define and redefine itself and its environment as open learning communities. The need to engage in this personal struggle to put open learning communities into practice in our own lives (both real and virtual), we are discovering, is essential to helping us develop our broader vision(s) of open learning communities. The strategy guiding the LWF unit in its work is derived from a tension that is continually being negotiated on the basis of an understanding of the complexity of different issues at stake, the bureaucracy that we work in, the institutions that we work with, the diverse environments that we operate in around the world and the constraints that we face. The strategy is also based on a understanding that we must attempt to situate ourselves and our activities at the edge of chaos, tenuously placing ourselves in a constant "push and pull" with the different systems that we are in contact with.

As a unit, we are involved in a fluid process of engaging in varying degrees of action and reflection along three inter-dependant layers of strategies and activities:

(1) conceptual inputs,

(2) policy and institutional capacity building, and

(3) pilot projects and field applications.

We very much see our role as trying to dynamically link research and practice, and practice and research. This, to a large degree, has involved both identifying and generating progressive opportunities as well as networking with inspiring partners both within existing formal and non-formal education systems as well as outside of them. We are continually looking for new projects that will help to elucidate and elaborate the concept and practice of open learning communities. Interestingly, LWF activities have thus far focused on areas which have tended to be regarded more at the fringe of conventional education systems e.g., certain forms of distance education, community schools, in-service teacher training, special needs education, and early childhood development. There has been greater flexibility in introducing and developing innovative approaches related to open learning communities in these domains.

LWF has also become heavily involved in activities centered around various information and communications technologies (ICTs) e.g., interactive radio and television, computers, and the Internet. These ICTs have considerable institutional and operational potential in shaking up rigid bureaucracies and changing organizational behavior, introducing spaces for raising questions and supporting dialogue, assisting people in seeing new realities, and transforming thinking and practice around learning. It should be clarified that we view technology as a tool for enabling and supporting open learning communities -- it is a means not an end. This being said, we are continually being confronted with the overwhelming nature of technology and are always struggling to keep technology from dominating our agenda. Partnerships are also a critical element in the development of LWF. A unique aspect of LWF is that it is envisioned as a non-proprietary concept i.e., that UNESCO does not 'own' it. With this understanding, the role of the LWF unit then is merely to provoke, stimulate, assist, facilitate, and connect with others interested in the concept.

Our challenge has been not to view different organizations as monolithic institutions, and treat them as such, but rather to identify exciting people and projects. Our growing number of committed partners today comprises dynamic individuals from governments, NGOs, universities, think/do tanks, international donors, various international networks, and private companies from around the world. The collective visions and activities of these partners ultimately define what LWF is and what it will become.

Recontextualising Teachers' Role

Teaching is essential to the learning process. However, conceptions about teaching and teachers have lagged behind and, as a result, often run counter to the changes required in response to the situations discussed above. The emphasis of the teaching process has been centered around the teacher rather than the learner. In recent history, the tendency has been to view the teacher as an impersonal "expert" in the classroom whose only role is to transmit knowledge, facts, skills to the "empty" learner.

The teacher is someone who intervenes in the learning process of others. The process can be seen as providing prompts for engaging, stimulating, structuring, and encouraging learning in individuals and communities. While transmission of some types of knowledge and skills is part of this process and will continue to be important, the complexity of society and demands made on the problem-solving capacity of human beings will require that teaching be seen as fundamentally going beyond the transmission of information. In the world of the future, we envision that the teacher will be responsible for carrying out several inter-connected roles, as briefly described below.

— *Facilitation*: Facilitating learning entails building, accessing and validating a variety of activities, frameworks, information, and experiences for the learner to connect to. It should be clarified that facilitation implies more than simply providing access to new information or technologies; rather, it involves enabling understanding and creating meaning. This means raising the capacity of learners to ask questions rather than focusing on the provision of answers to predetermined questions. The teacher must challenge the thoughts and ideas of learners and stimulate them to engage in critical thinking and self-reflection. Essential to the process of facilitation is the ability of the teacher to link the appropriate set of interactions with the individual learning styles, interests and experiences of each learner as well as with the profiles of the communities that the learners perceive themselves as being part of.

— *Curriculum Innovation*: Centralized curricula around the world have often been unable to take into account the rich diversity in society and suffered from lack of imagination, flexibility and relevance. The result is that many learners find themselves "lost" in the learning process. Given the broad range of learning styles, needs, interests, backgrounds, and aspirations of learners, teachers must adapt and develop new curricular approaches, content and language to ensure that curricula are, on one level, linked to the daily life of the learner but, on another level, push the learners to.8 explore beyond the mundane aspects of their daily lives into undiscovered possibilities. The movement towards decentralization provides an opportunity for allowing teachers greater control over the curricula. However, with curriculum innovation, there must be greater efforts to conduct decentralized and participatory field research in order to understand the strengths and weaknesses of different strategies.

Engaging in such research allows teachers to interact constructively and flexibly with the curriculum on a continual basis.

— *Connection of Learners and Communities*: While learning is an individualized effort, it is also a social activity. Teaching must be conceived of in terms of a larger social exercise of connecting learners (and, in the process, building communities) to each other and to the world around them. The process of connecting learners involves creating dialogue among diverse groups of learners that allow them to understand and appreciate the differences as well as the similarities that bond us as human beings. This means that teachers must be committed to understanding their learners and the communities that they come from. As part of this on-going process, they must also be willing to question their own internal biases and stereotypes.

— *Complementing/Supplementing Other Channels*: In addition to the traditional teacher, many other additional "channels" currently exist and are emerging, such as textbooks, newspapers, and magazines, educational radio or TV broadcasts, computers, audio or video tapes, the surrounding physical and human environment, libraries, specialized work areas such as to perform science experiments or for creative expression. Teaching becomes a process of integrating these resources so that they complement, supplement and enhance each other. This demands a sensitivity to the inherent strengths and weaknesses of each of the channels and how they satisfy to different styles of learning and different types of content. Teachers can also play a role in introducing these new media into communities where there is often fear or resistance to change.

— *Motivational Support:* The teacher must play a critical role in providing motivational support through constructive feedback and encouragement to the learner, responding to a broad range of motivational needs that vary over time and across learners. Learning is a process that is filled with success and failure — oftentimes involving great struggle and perseverance on the part of the learner. In many cases, failure can lead to great disappointment and withdrawal. However, if well managed, failure can also be turned into an important prompt to learning and thus can become the basis for success. It is the role of the teacher to provide positive inspiration at critical junctures of the learning process to ensure that learners stick with the laborious task of learning. However, the teacher should not take on this role in isolation, but rather seek to.9 build a learning community in which other learners provide motivational support to each other as well.

— *Learning*: A good teacher is a continual learner. In order to be effective, the teacher must remain connected with changing societal frames of reference (economic, cultural, political, social, technological, etc.) as well as with changing needs and interests of learners. They must be able to learn from their environment. But more importantly, they must be able to learn from their learners. This involves constantly trying to understand how learners react to, interpret and create meaning from different activities. It also involves a willingness to experiment with and adapt new approaches. In addition, the process of teaching involves modeling a love of learning. This love is something that one cannot fake. If the teacher demonstrates a dedication to learning, there is a high probability that the learners will "catch" that spirit of learning.

We are all teachers just as we are all learners. The implications of the discussion in the previous sections points to a situation in which teaching can no longer be considered the sole jurisdiction or responsibility of the traditional classroom teacher. The teacher in the institution we call 'schools' still has an important role to play in supporting the learning process. However, we must seek to break down the barriers that have supported the historical isolation of teachers in schools from other "teachers" in society. In order for continuous learning to occur, the responsibility for teaching must be distributed and integrated with other institutions and individuals in throughout society. We thus posit three broad categories of "teachers":

— *Human beings*: This category includes the teacher in the classroom. But it also includes a wider range of individuals in society who are informally called upon to play equally important roles in complementing/supplementing the classroom teacher. These "teachers" build alternative learning environments and mediate access to diverse and valuable bodies of knowledge, traditions, information, skills, experiences, etc. The profound teaching contributions made by such groups as parents, family members, friends; community and religious leaders; literacy, community health, agricultural extension workers; tutors in different distance learning settings; journalists, artists, actors, musicians; media people; and, artisans, craftsmen, farmers, traders, should be validated. In addition, we should recognize that learners are oftentimes teachers as they are called upon in many occasions to contribute to the learning of others.

— *Media*: The "teacher" should also be seen as including a variety of media for the learner to connect to. Such media-constructed environments include those that are built around technology and take the form of print, television, radio, computers, etc. It also includes learning that is prompted by socio-cultural activities such as community service activities, meditation/prayer, internships/ apprenticeships, etc. In addition, one cannot overlook the learning that takes place when one is able to connect with the natural environment. We must clarify though that while the human "teacher" will be a medium among the other media, the human teacher is still distinct from these other media with roles and attributes that cannot be substituted by them, particularly in the sense that only the human teacher is capable of engaging in learning him or herself.

— *Life experience*: We are also taught by life experiences. This includes spontaneous processes such as love and death, that cannot be easily structured or planned in a conscious way. It also includes processes that are determined, at least to an extent, by choice or by the dynamics of the human environment the individual is part of. It is thus a crucial task of human as well as mediated teachers to connect learners to such important channels of learning, helping them to reflect on and value their experience, and to integrate life experience with the curriculum.

Learning is a natural human process that occurs wherever human beings interact with each other and with their environments. Much of society's effort to create the conditions for learning concentrate on the school system. However, learning can take place in formal as well as informal settings. It is not uncommon that some of the best instances of learning occur outside a formal setting as the learners tend to be more at ease and learning tends to be more contextualized within a relevant socio-cultural setting. For learning both within and outside the formal context to become optimally effective, it is thus important that artificial barriers between the two environments be reduced. Different media can play an important role in bridging the gap.

The area of teacher education provides a natural starting point for initiating this process of change. However, as we will highlight hereafter, it should be clear from the onset that teacher education is an integrated part of a broader conception encompassing the education of both learners and teachers for their new roles in open learning communities. In this section, then, we will discuss points of intervention into teacher education, particularly focusing on how information and communication technologies can be used to facilitate the process of change. But first it is necessary to reframe a few key conceptions around teacher education. The emergence of new ICTs provides an opportunity and a necessity for pursuing this exercise.

The distinction between pre-service and in-service education is no longer a useful one. This is particularly the case if we begin to conceive of teacher education in terms of a more continuous and fluid process. In this context, pre-service teacher education is best to be seen as a preparation not only for a pre-determined role as teacher but particularly also for effective interaction with a continued learning-teaching process. The new ICTs help negotiate a hybridization between formal and distance education so that face-to-face teaching is no longer only for the pre-service education and distance education is no longer only reserved for in-service education. Throughout the teacher education process, there should be a strong integration of both face-to-face and distance learning approaches.

Perraton defines distance education as "an educational process in which a significant proportion of the teaching is conducted by someone removed in space and time from the learner." However, such a definition begins to rapidly lose its meaning if we situate it within the broader construct of learning and teaching discussed previously. The more it becomes an established notion that the teacher engages in learning and the learner is a teaching agent, the less relevant it becomes to focus on the separation in space and time of the two roles. The relationship between teaching and learning is fundamentally a dialectical one, based on a partnership between human beings to jointly create meaning. This partnership is no longer solely dependent on the physical proximity of its constituent members, nor is its quality necessarily determined by it. Separation in space and time is a mere matter of option, in many cases based on convenience or appropriateness in context rather than sheer necessity. What matters, and what needs to be validated, is simply the quality of the dialogue between partners "teachers" and "learners" in the traditional sense of the word, but also other members of the learning community.

"Teacher/learners", as they emerge from their traditional roles, must now first of all learn to become good learners. Being a good learner is not an easy task — it requires a great deal of discipline, patience, resourcefulness, inquisitiveness, open-mindedness, creativity and flexibility. This implies that teacher education must put greater emphasis on developing in "teacher/learners" the skills required to become better learners. In addition to encouraging teachers to become learners, teacher education must also support the process of "learner/teachers" in becoming teachers, both in terms of how they can teach each other and how they can teach the teacher. Thus, teacher education may seek to involve "learner/teachers" in parts of the process.

The new ICTs must not be viewed as replacing the human element in teacher education. There is increased frustration with the existing process of teacher education. ICTs are sometimes seen as a means of "fixing" this problem, particularly as they allow bypassing — or doing away altogether with — the assumed weak link, the traditional teacher trainer. This view, however, is erroneous. It was argued above that, in a context of different media, including the human being as one of them, the most striking characteristic which distinguishes the human medium from non-human ones, is the capacity to learn. "Teacher/learners" can thus best be prepared for their new roles in an environment which models the behaviours they are expected to acquire. Such an environment should therefore be profoundly human and humanizing and technologies need to be incorporated in it so as to enhance, rather than to detract from, this human aspect.

Many attempts at improving the quality and motivation of "teacher/learners" through teacher training schemes have resulted in disappointment. Evaluations point, among other weaknesses, to the cascade model and its inherent transmission loss as well as to the gap between what is learned in the training situation and the realities of the field. The use of information and communication technologies within a distance learning context is often advocated as a way to overcome such weaknesses. Excitement has been generated around new ICTs as it is assumed that they can 'bring the best expert directly to the teacher' and facilitate two-way communication between the teacher and learner. Unfortunately, these are very narrow applications of the ICTs and we do not foresee them to result in any significant shifts in learning and teaching as they are simply extensions of existing approaches and processes. These "benefits" only serve to reinforce the teacher-over-learner hierarchies. However, the ICTs, if properly applied, possess the ability to unleash revolutionary changes in the field of teacher education. We suggest the following focal points for application of the new ICTs to teacher education.

Teacher education should be geared towards building a link between the various "teacher/learners" in society. Selected joint training sessions may be organized to do this with ICTs being utilized to facilitate greater communication, collaboration and reflection among the various partners. Initial sessions could start with discussions on how to work together, sharing of roles, and ensuring overlap (for reinforced learning). Such a process of dialogue should be geared towards discovering a basis for partnership in building open learning communities i.e., identifying strengths and weaknesses of each partner, formulating an understanding of the needs and interests of various learners, negotiating points of compromise, and team building. More importantly, it should be focused on developing a shared consensus around learning and how it relates to broader objectives of social change and development. In addition, the ICTs provide an interesting opportunity for involving "learner/teachers" in selected teacher education activities. They can play a role in facilitating increased communication and sharing between "teacher/learners" and "learner/teachers." The ICTs potentially provide a way for not only the "learner/teacher" to understand the "teacher/learner" better but also for the "teacher/learner" to understand the "learner/teacher" and for the "learner/teachers" to understand each other, and sometimes even themselves, better.

One of the strengths of the ICTs is that they facilitate moving away from generic teacher education models with relatively little relevance to the lives and daily problems of the "teacher/learner." The ICTs allow for the development of specific training models that are sensitive to the different needs, working conditions, learning styles, language and backgrounds of individual "teacher/learners." Such individually-tailored approaches of teacher education are better geared towards addressing issues of motivation and morale. However, this should not be taken to mean that a group of centralized training designers try to design hundreds of specialized training programs, but rather that they should utilize the ICTs to support a process in which "teacher/learners" take on a greater role in generating and designing their own training programs.

The ICTs allow the potential for teacher education to be moved out of centralized training institutions and into the "teacher/learner's" own working environment. In addition, they open up the opportunity to think of teacher education as a career-long career-wide activity rather than as a pre-service phase with bouts of in-service training merely for refresher purposes. Such an emphasis on on-going training is essential to allowing the "teacher/ learners" to continually reflect on critical aspects of their own teaching as well as critical aspects of their own learning.

The ICTs allow us to rethink the content of teacher education. Traditionally there has been an artificial dichotomy between mastery of subject matter and pedagogical/andragogical skills, sometimes with a tendency for teacher education to emphasize the subject matter aspect of the content. Teacher education content should be re-oriented to focus on learning and learners with subject matter and pedagogical/andragogical elements integrated around this focus. In addition, the ICTs should be used to make teacher education more consistent with the pedagogical/andragogical concerns being advocated, such as active learning, critical thinking, collaborative processes and creativity.

Noting the expanding role the new media are already playing in the provision of education and cognizant of how this role will undoubtedly expand, it is critical to recognize the importance of media literacy among "teacher/learners." Such media literacy requires a strong understanding of the strengths and limitations of each medium and familiarity with strategies to reinforce the effect one medium can have on learning through the use of other media. However, the idea of media literacy should be conceived beyond the glitzy hi-tech schemes available on the market. "Old" technologies such as print, radio, television will no doubt continue to make great contributions to the development of open learning environments world-wide, particularly if integrated in supporting community contexts. Furthermore, the "teacher/learner" should be encouraged venture beyond them and also make improved use of relatively unexplored media of popular expression such as puppet shows, local dances and music. Teacher education should ensure that teachers interact and experiment with these various media and creatively reflect upon how they can best be used in different learning environments. This should be more than a mere theoretical exercise and actually involve hands-on experience.

6

Distance Learning and Copyright Issues

A copyright grants the holder the sole right to reproduce or grant permission to others to reproduce the copyrighted works. The copyright holder is defined as the person who owns the exclusive rights to a work. The protection is limited to original works, whether or not they have been published. However, it is the expression of the idea that is copyrighted, not the idea in and of itself. Copyright may be held on a variety of original works which include: literary works, musical works, dramatic works, graphical works, motion pictures, sound recordings, and architectural works. The Copyright Law of 1976 defined the right of the copyright holder, items that may be copyrighted, fair use guidelines, etc. The right to a work may be used, sold, or given away as the copyright holder deems appropriate. The exclusive rights provided for in the Act (17 USC section 106) include:

— to reproduce the copyrighted work in any format;

— to prepare derivative works;

— to distribute copies of the copyrighted work to the public by sale, rent, lease, or gift;

— to perform the copyrighted work publicly (in the case of plays, musical recordings, movies, etc.); and

— to display the copyrighted work publicly (in the case of literary, musical, pictorial, graphic works, etc.)

The concept of "fair use" was established in the Copyright Law of 1976. It specifies situations in which copyrighted materials may be used without express permission of the copyright holder (17 USC section 107). However, with the technology available today, it is very easy to abuse the "fair use" provision.

The US House of Representatives suggested that the three major considerations in determining fair use should be: brevity of the selection, spontaneity of the decision, and the cumulative effect of the use of the selection. Section 107 of the Copyright Law lists four factors that define "fair use" (17 USC section 107):

— The purpose and character of the use must be educational or non profit in nature.

— The nature of the copyrighted work.

— Copied material must be an excerpt or a portion of the original work without being a critical portion.

— The teacher may not impair the marketability of the work. This is the most difficult condition to determine and is the most controversial.

Publishers and educators agreed to more specific guidelines which will provide a list of safe parameters in which colleges may operate. However, if a college exceeds the guidelines, they will open themselves to a lawsuit to challenge the use as fair. Congress never agreed to these guidelines, but since they were established by a diverse group of educators and copyright holders, courts tend to recognize their validity.

The guidelines also require that the copying be for only one course, and no more than one short poem, article, or story or two excerpts can be copied from the works of any one author. Lastly, all copied materials MUST show the original copyright notice from the work. There are also several prohibitions related to fair use. These are guidelines, and are not the law.

— Unauthorized copying may not be used to replace an anthology or compilation.

— Unauthorized copies may not be made of consumable works such as workbooks or standardized tests.

— Unauthorized copying may not substitute for the purchase of books, authorized reprints, or periodicals.

— Unauthorized copying may not be directed by a higher authority, such as a department head or dean.

— The same instructor may not copy the same item without permission from term to term.

— Students cannot be charged beyond the actual cost of photocopying.

Copyright permission must be obtained from the copyright holder of the work in which you are interested. However, copyright nctice is optional for works published on or after March 1, 1989, so tracking down the copyright holder may be difficult. When requesting copyright permission, include all of the following information:

— Full name(s) of the author, editor, and/or translator;

— Title, edition, and volume number of the work;

— Copyright date of the work;

— ISBN for books or ISSN for magazines;

— Exact pages, figures, and illustrations you wish to use;

— The number of copies to be made;

— If the material will be used alone or in combination with other works;

— Name of the college or university;

— Date when the material will be used; and

— Instructor's full name, address, and telephone number.

As distance educators, preparing multimedia presentations is a viable teaching strategy. In doing so, the instructor must keep in mind some basic principles:

— Combining content from other sources can be copyright protected.

— Original multimedia works are copyrighted.

Educators have always utilized outside resources to enhance the learning experience for their students. These resources can range from a newspaper clipping to a book to a movie. All of these items, and many other resources, are copyrighted materials. The Copyright Law of 1976 established the rights of the copyright holder as well as providing for the use of copyrighted materials, especially in educational settings. In order to comply with the law in the area of copyright and proper use of copyrighted materials, educators must be aware of the law and the parameters that govern proper or "fair use" of copyrighted publications. There are both civil and criminal penalties for infringement of copyright law.

Civil awards generally include a monetary award of up to $1,000,000, attorney fees, an injunction against the violator, and confiscation of the materials that used the copyrighted works. Distance educators have a unique dilemma when dealing with copyright law. Due to the time that the law was passed and the rapid advancement of technology for distance education, the provisions for education in the copyright law are often unclear for the distance education classroom.

Distance learning promises students in remote areas, those with family responsibilities who cannot attend classes offered at regular times, and persons employed full-time the educational opportunities many have long sought.

Distance learning also holds tremendous excitement for faculty members and for educational institutions that seek to meet the needs of underserved populations. Institutions and faculty members are working to determine what delivery mechanisms and instructional methodologies best facilitate teaching and learning for these students.

Librarians are trying to decide how to provide distance learners with the research and study materials they need. In the United States, copyright law often proves to be an impediment to distance learning, and no one is sure how fair use will be extended to remote instruction in the digital age.

Providing library services to distance learners under the existing copyright law may be easier than the offering of courses and degree programs generally. What works well in the traditional classroom with face-to-face teaching may not be so successful for different levels of students in all types of distance learning offerings. Teachers must be able to experiment with various forms of instruction and to utilize the full array of technological advances to deliver courses at the convenience of the student. While educational institutions test different delivery mechanisms and methodologies, the technology continues to advance.

In the United States copyright law focuses on how the limitations and exemptions to that law found in Section 107 (fair use), Section 110(1) (the classroom exemption) and Section 110(2) (instructional broadcasting) affect distance education.

Despite many educators' wishes, it is not at all clear that the use of copyrighted works permitted in face-to-face teaching is permitted for distance learning. Currently, there are pending amendments that would redefine the meaning of face-to-face teaching in U.S. law to make it much easier to use copyrighted works in distance learning to parallel uses in the traditional classroom.

The Copyright Act, 17 U.S.C. Sections 101-1101 (1994) recognizes the unique position and importance of education by providing crucial exemptions to the exclusive rights of the copyright holder. Both tradition and Congress support the notion that teaching and learning occupy a unique place in our society such that using copyrighted works in education may trump even the exclusive rights of copyright owners.

Section 106 of the Copyright Act gives copyright holders a bundle of five rights: reproduction, distribution, adaptation, performance and display. Referred to as the exclusive rights, fortunately for educators and students, several subsequent sections of the Act restrict the exclusive rights of the copyright holder. The most important of these limitations is Section 107, fair use. Fair use is a privilege that permits one other than the copyright owner to reproduce, distribute, adapt, perform or display a work; in other words, activities that otherwise would be within the exclusive rights of the copyright holder.

The Act states that despite the grant of exclusive rights under Section 106, "...[T]he fair use of a copyrighted work, including such use by reproduction in copies or phonorecords or any other means specified by that section for purposes such as criticism, comment, news reporting, teaching (including multiple copying for classroom use), scholarship or research, is not an infringement of copyright." Thus, teaching is mentioned directly in the text of Section 107. The section then lists four factors that a court will consider in determining whether a use is a fair use. The factors include: (1) purpose and character of the use, (2) nature of the copyrighted work, (3) amount and substantiality of the use, and (4) nature of the copyrighted work.

Section 110 in the Copyright act provides important exemptions for nonprofit educational institutions. Section 110(1), referred to as the "classroom exemption," is one of the best exemptions provided in U.S. copyright law. It provides an absolute exemption to the exclusive rights of the copyright holder for performances and displays in the classroom if certain conditions are met.

The performance or display must be in the course of face-to-face teaching, in a classroom, and, if the work performed is a motion picture or other audiovisual work, the copy must have been lawfully made. There is no restriction on the types of works that are included. Although "classroom" is broadly defined to include any place where instruction is occurring such as laboratories, gymnasiums and libraries when the class comes to the library, the face-to-face restriction excludes distance learning from this particular exemption.

Section 110(2) covers distance learning, but it is much more restrictive than 110(1). When the Act was passed in 1976, the only type of distance learning that Congress envisioned involved television technology. Today, one might consider this to mean transmitting rather than just instructional broadcasting.

While Section 110(1) is very broad, in contrast, Section 110(2) is quite narrow. First, only certain types of works may be performed, specifically nondramatic literary and musical works may be transmitted for distance learning, although any work may be displayed. Second, the transmission of the performance or display must be part of the systematic instructional activities of the institution. Third, reception must be in a classroom or other place similarly devoted to instruction, although disabled persons may receive the transmission anywhere if their condition prevents attendance at a regular classroom. Fourth, the performance must be directly related and of material assistance to the teaching content of the transmission. Each of these four conditions causes difficulty for modern distance learning.

It is counterintuitive to teachers that they can use a videotape in face-to-face teaching without seeking permission from the copyright holder, but if that same course is offered to distance learners, use of the tape requires that permission be sought and royalties be paid if the copyright owner requests payment. It seems particularly silly if the course is offered to students face-to-face in a classroom and is simultaneously transmitted to distance learners. Yet, this is exactly what the Act requires.

Many schools currently seek permission and pay fees to use videotapes for distance learning. Some schools simply black out the time for distance learners when a tape is being shown to students in the classroom. Others probably ignore the law. The argument made by copyright holders is that absent distance learning courses, they would have sold individual copies of their works to the receiving sites. Thus, owners lose sales and should be compensated in the form of royalties for performances of their works outside of that permitted by Section 110(2).

Today most distance learning courses are received in a classroom which meets the requirements of the statute. Further, there are educators who believe that there should be a teacher at the receiving site to direct class discussion, etc. Despite this, classrooms are not likely to remain the dominant place for reception of such programs, especially as online courses are developed.

Currently, many educational institutions offer distance learning courses through television technology, and reception of that programming is in the home. Reception of courses in the home by non-disabled learners does not comply with the requirements in the Act. There are also questions about whether works like background qualify as being directly related to and of material assistance to the teaching content of the course. Displays that illustrate particular points of the lecture clearly are related, but if the instructor chooses art work that simply decorates or adds visual interest, it may not so qualify.

In 1997, Senate Bill 1146, the Digital Copyright Clarification and Technology Education Act was introduced in September by Senator Ashcroft. In November, the Boucher-Campbell bill, House Bill 3048, the Digital Era Copyright Enhancement Act, was introduced. Although not identical, both bills include provisions that will aid distance learning. They state directly that neither the means by which a work has been performed, displayed or distributed nor the application of an effective technological measure affects fair use.

Neither bill gives the education community a blank check for distance learning, but they do make it clear that distance learning is not limited to analog broadcast and closed circuit television. Both bills would amend Section 110(2) by adding the word "distribution" to performance and display of a work. Further, the limitation on the types of works that may be used for distance learning and on the place of reception are removed. Passage of these bills would considerably facilitate teaching for distance learning courses and remove many of the copyright restrictions that impede distributed education.

On the other hand, these bills do not give institutions a free hand; they will continue to pay license fees for reproducing works, for producing coursepacks for distance learners whether in print or digital format and for the use of works that are not directly related to the teaching content of the transmission. Major library associations, including the American Library Association, along with the Digital Future Coalition, have urged librarians and others not only to support this legislation but also to contact their congressional representatives to encourage their support and signing on as co-sponsors of the bills.

If an online course contains all of the materials a student needs for the course, and if the copyright for some of that materials is not owned by the teacher or the institution offering the course, it is unlikely that the provisions of Section 110(2) or even fair use can be met. Such a course is more similar to the old correspondence-type course. If the online course contains the full text of an article or other copyrighted work, then the work is reproduced each time a student taking the course downloads the work or prints it. If the course contains the performance of a videotape, the performance is outside the confines of the existing Section 110(2) exemption. Further, the tape is duplicated each time a student copies the work in order to view it on a television. Should the work be viewed or performed on the computer screen, there is still an argument that duplication into the computer's RAM is a reproduction that triggers the copyright owner's exclusive rights. Whether such temporary copies constitute a reproduction has not been finally determined, and there are cases that go both ways. Both the Ashcroft and Boucher-Campbell bills would exempt incidental copies such as those in RAM as bẹing transitory and not a part of the copyright owner's exclusive rights.

Libraries in nonprofit educational institutions are fortunate in that they can treat students who are taking distance learning courses as primary clientele. In order for a library to qualify for the library exemption, it must meet three requirements:

(i) the reproduction and distribution must not be for direct or indirect commercial advantage,

(ii) the library must be open to the public or to researchers doing research in the same or a similar field and

(iii) the copies must contain a notice of copyright.

Thus, upon the request from a distance learner, the library can give him or her a copy of a single article from a periodical issue or a chapter of a book under Section 108(d) if the copy becomes the property of the user, the library has no notice that the copy will be used for other than fair use purposes and the library provides the Register of Copyright's warning as mandated. Most libraries maintain that they may also provide an electronic copy of an article to a user as long as the copy meets the requirements of Section 108(d) including that the library does not retain the electronic copy. Should the article be one from an electronic journal to which the library subscribes, then the weight of authority appears to be that the license agreement controls whether a copy may be provided to students not physically present on the campus.

According to Section 108(f)(4) of the Copyright Act, nothing "in any way affects...any contractual obligations assumed at any time by the library...when it obtained a copy...of a work in its collection." Clearly, in negotiating licenses for full-text journals and other materials, libraries should insist that access to any student enrolled in a course offered by that institution be permitted access under the terms of the license. At the request of individual faculty members, libraries maintain reserve collections of photocopied materials for courses. These consist of materials developed by the faculty member as well as copies of copyrighted articles, book chapters, etc. Copies of these materials may be provided to distance learners under the same conditions that they are made available to on-campus students. However, libraries should note that under the 1982 ALA Model Policy for Reserve Collections, materials photocopied for reserve should not constitute all of the materials for a course. This would represent a coursepack, and two important court decisions have indicated that permission should be sought and royalties paid for coursepacks. As libraries develop electronic reserve collections, they should develop policies that conform with fair use. Further, in establishing such systems, libraries can ensure that distance learners have access to materials it has digitized for reserves.

Copyright law and Promotion of Distance Education

In order to determine whether changes in the law are advisable to promote distance education through digital technologies, it is necessary to examine current laws. Copyright laws protects original works of authorship, including literature, movies, plays, computer programs, music, works of art and sound recordings. Copyright confers on the owner a bundle of exclusive rights to make or authorize certain uses of the work:

(1) to reproduce it in copies or phonorecords;

(2) to prepare derivative works (such as adaptions. or translations);

(3) to distribute copies to the public;

(4) to perform the work publicly, limited in the case of sound recordings to performances by means of a digital audio transmission; and

(5) to display the work publicly.

These rights are divisible, and may be licensed or sold together or separately. The exercise of any of the exclusive rights in a copyrighted work without the authorization of the copyright owner is an infringement, unless an exception applies.

The US Copyright Act contains numerous exceptions, including several that are particularly relevant to educational uses.Different rights are implicated by different educational activities, depending in part on the technologies used. A teacher using a work to teach her class will almost invariably exercise one or more of the copyright owner's exclusive rights, when she reads from a work, displays it, or reproduces it and hands out copies. This is true whether the instruction is face-to-face, or takes place over a distance.

A public performance or display of a work accomplished by means of a digital transmission, however, may implicate additional exclusive rights in a manner not contemplated by the instructor or perceived by the student. Unlike face-to-face teaching or broadcasting, acts perceived by the teacher and student as a performance or display of work, when transmitted over a digital network, will generally constitute an exercise of the reproduction right, and possibly the distribution right as well.

Digital transmissions can be grouped into two categories for the purposes of this analysis: those that involve the automatic creation of copies during the transmission process, and those that do not. The first kind of digital transmission involves communication via a computer network. When material is transmitted to a distant location over a computer network, temporary RAM copies are made in the computers through which it passes, by virtue of the technological process of transmission. The copy of the work that arrives on the recipient's computer is the ultimate copy in this process. This is an essential function of the way that digital information is transported over a digital network.

In addition to the necessary transient copies generated in the course of transmitting the performance or display, the reproduction right may be exercised in connection with a networked computer transmission in other ways. For material that is not in digital form, making a digital copy from the analog version also entails an exercise of the copyright owner's reproduction right. When a teacher scans a work into a computer, the reproduction right is implicated. Also, a student could make temporary or permanent copies by caching, downloading or printing out the material after receipt.

The distribution right is also implicated when a transmission results in a distribution of copies to the public. As a result of almost every digital transmission, a temporary copy is deposited on the recipient's computer, as well as, possibly, more permanent copies. The second kind of digital transmission is exemplified by digital television or radio transmissions, which may be communicated by satellite, microwave, or cable. These transmissions do not involve the automatic creation of intermediate copies. Therefore, from a copyright perspective, they are more similar to analog broadcasts than to online transmissions.

The fact that an educational use implicates one or more of the copyright owner's exclusive rights does not necessarily mean that the use is an infringement. Only unauthorized uses can infringe, and permission to use the work may be expressly granted or implied. The copyright owner, either the author or the author's transferee, can grant permission through an express license. An educator may contact the copyright owner, or a licensing organization acting on her behalf, to obtain a license to use the work.

Even without such permission, courts may imply from a copyright owner's conduct an intent to allow the work to be used in a certain way, creating an implied license. Applying this doctrine, certain educational uses could be found to be authorized by implication. For instance, a copyright owner who posts his work on a website without restriction may have impliedly licensed users to access the work in order to view it, including the making of those temporary reproductions required to do so. Such an implied license may be of limited utility to distance educators, because it would not authorize making or distributing other types of copies for use in a class. If express or implied permission is not granted, the use of a copyrighted work may still be lawful if it falls within one of the various exceptions to the copyright owner's exclusive rights.

The US Copyright Act contains a number of exceptions to the copyright owner's rights, permitting various uses without the need to obtain a license. The two main exemptions specifically designed for educators are provisions relating to face-to-face classroom teaching and instructional broadcasting, contained in section 110 of the Act. The fair use doctrine is the third major exemption applicable to educational uses. This section analyzes these three exemptions, which together largely define the scope of permitted uses for digital distance education. It also discusses several other provisions of the Copyright Act which allow a distance educator to make certain limited uses of a copyrighted work.

In the 1976 Copyright Act, US Congress provided two specific exemptions from the exclusive rights of a copyright owner for certain types of educational performances and displays. In order to understand their genesis and purpose, some background is useful. Prior copyright law limited the public performance right in nondramatic literary and musical works to performances that were "for profit." The right to perform dramatic works was broader, without the for-profit limitation. There was no general equivalent to the display right, however, and so no distinction between for-profit or nonprofit displays.

During the years of the revision process leading up to the 1976 Act, there was pressure from a number of groups, including the educational community, to continue and expand the "blanket exemption" approach to permit all nonprofit performances of any work. This approach was ultimately rejected, in favor of providing general public performance and display rights in all works, whether or not exercised for profit, subject to exemptions for particular types of performances and displays "that by their nature justify being exempted from copyright control." In explaining the shift to general rights with specific exemptions, the Register of Copyrights stated that "the present blanket exemption has become too broad in its applicationto the new conditions of today, and . . . would involve serious dangers to the author's rights if continued into the future."

Two of the new specific exemptions addressed the use of works in the course of nonprofit educational instruction, reflecting general consensus that instructional uses justified a degree of special treatment under the copyright law. One addressed face-to-face classroom teaching, while the other addressed instructional broadcasting. In the legislative history of section 110, Congress stated that "[c]lauses (1) and (2) between them are intended to cover all of the various methods by which performances or displays in the course of systematic instruction take place."

Together with the doctrine of fair use, these provisions have essentially governed the range of exempted instructional uses for over twenty years. (a) Section 110(1). Section 110(1) exempts the performance or display of any work in the course of face-to-face teaching activities. By its terms, it does not apply to any distance education uses. It permits: performance or display of a work by instructors or pupils in the course of face-to-face teaching activities of a nonprofit educational institution, in a classroom or similar place devoted to instruction, unless, in the case of a motion picture or other audiovisual work, the performance, or the display of individual images, is given by means of a copy that was not lawfully made under this title, and that the person responsible for the performance knew or had reason to believe was not lawfully made.

According to the then—Register of Copyrights, section 110(1) reflects "general agreement that most ordinary instructional activities in classrooms should be exempt from copyright control." The potentially broad coverage of this exemption caused some concern to copyright owners, and the drafters therefore included a number of limiting factors to confine the permitted uses to purely instructional ones.One limitation is that the performance or display must be made in the course of "face-to- face teaching activities," which the legislative history explicitly states excludes educational broadcasts or transmissions.

The performance or display must also be made in a "classroom or similar place devoted to instruction," which, according to the legislative history, excludes auditoriums used for school plays, graduations or school assemblies, but includes libraries, auditoriums or workshops used as classrooms in the course of systematic instructional activities.

The exemption was intended to extend, however, beyond the physical classroom itself to situations where the instructor and students are "in the same building or general area," and devices for amplifying or reproducing sound, or projecting visual images, are used. Another limitation is that the exemption only applies to the teaching activities of "a nonprofit educational institution." This parallels the prior law's differentiation between for-profit and nonprofit performances, discussed above, and excludes "performances or displays in profit-making institutions such as dance studios and language schools."Finally, section 110(1) is limited in the rights that it covers. It exempts only the performance or display of a work-the major ways in which a teacher would use works while engaged in face-to-face instruction. It does not authorize their reproduction or distribution, or the creation of derivative works.

A proposal to limit section 110(2) to closed-circuit, on-campus broadcasts was considered but rejected as too narrow. Ultimately, the scope applied to both open or closed-circuit broadcasting technologies, as long as the other requirements of the exemption were met. Section 110(2) authorizes:

performance of a nondramatic literary or musical work or display of a work, by or in the course of a transmission, if -

(A) the performance or display is a regular part of the systematic instructional activities of a governmental body or a nonprofit educational institution; and

(B) the performance or display is directly related and of material assistance to the teaching content of the transmission; and

(C) the transmission is made primarily for-

(i) reception in classrooms or similar places normally devoted to instruction, or

(ii) reception by persons to whom the transmission is directed because their disabilities or other special circumstances prevent their attendance in classrooms or similar places normally devoted to instruction, or

(iii) reception by officers or employees of governmental bodies as a part of their official duties or employment.

Like section 110(1), section 110(2) exempts only acts of performance and display. It does not authorize reproduction, distribution or the making of derivative works. It is narrower than section 110(1), however, in the categories of works it covers. While it permits displays of all works, it permits performances only of nondramatic literary or musical works. Thus, an instructor would not be able under this section to project a movie or perform a play via an educational broadcast.

During the revision process, educational groups had argued that the public interest in education would be furthered if the exemption permitted the performance of all types of works. However, the Register recommended maintaining the traditional distinction between dramatic and nondramatic works, exempting nonprofit performances only for the latter. The justification for the distinction was discussed in the US Register's Report on the revision of the copyright law. The Register noted that copyright owners have had a general right of public performance in dramatic works since 1856, while the right to perform nondramatic works had always been limited to for-profit performances.

The exclusion of performances of dramatic works thus recognizes that instructional broadcasts are more likely to supplant the intended market for such works. Audiovisual works, many of which are similarly dramatic in nature, were also excluded from the exemption. Nor is the performance of sound recordings authorized by section 110(2). This is not due to concerns about market impact, but rather because there was no exclusive right at the time for any type of performance of sound recordings, and therefore no need for an exemption. Section 110(2) also contains limitations on the nature and content of the transmission, and the identity and location of the recipients.

First, the performance or display must be made as a regular part of systematic instructional activity by a nonprofit educational institution or governmental body. According to the legislative history, the concept of "systematic instructional activity" was "intended as the general equivalent of 'curriculums,' but it could be broader in a case such as that of an institution using systematic teaching methods not related to specific course work." Although the educational institution must be nonprofit, as in section 110(1), Congress indicated that "[t]he use of commercial facilities, such as those of a cable service, to transmit the performance or display, would not affect the exemption as long as the actual performance or display was for nonprofit purposes."

Second, the performance or display must be directly related, and of material assistance, to the teaching content. This test of relevance and materiality connects the copyrighted work to the curriculum. It would rule out the section's applicability to the use of a work for entertainment purposes, such as background music used simply to embellish the lesson.Similarly, if more of the work is used than is material to the subject taught, in order to make the class more appealing or attractive, the additional use may not qualify.

Third, the exemption provides certain restrictions on where the transmission can be received and who the recipients can be. The recipients must be located in a classroom or similar place of instruction, or they must be persons "to whom the transmission is directed because their disabilities or other special circumstances prevent their attendance in classrooms." Legislative history indicates that "special circumstances" could include the inability of university students to take standard daytime classes because of work or other commitments:

There has been some question as to whether or not the language in this section of the bill is intended to include instructional television college credit courses. These telecourses are aimed at undergraduate and graduate students in earnest pursuit of higher educational degrees who are unable to attend daytime classes because of daytime employment, distance from campus, or some other intervening reason. So long as these broadcasts are aimed at regularly enrolled students and conducted by recognized higher educational institutions, the committee believes that they are clearly within the language of section 110 (2)©(ii).

Like night school and correspondence courses before them, these telecourses are fast becoming a valuable adjunct of the normal college curriculum.The transmission must be made primarily, but not solely, for reception by these persons. "[T]he transmission could still be exempt even though it is capable of reception by the public at large. . . . Factors to consider in determining the 'primary' purpose of a program would include its subject matter, content, and the time of its transmission." This flexibilitywas necessary because, using the technologies available, including open-circuit broadcasting, there was no practical way to ensure that the educational broadcasts reached only eligible students.

Taken together, these limitations, which exceed those in section 110(1), represent an attempt to balance the benefits and risks inherent in the practice of instructional broadcasting. Addressing this provision, the Register of Copyrights stated that "it . . . cannot be denied that educational broadcasting is in a special category. Its general aim is public and community service, and some of its instructional activities are essentially an extension, to a larger audience, of what schools have been doing for centuries." However, in explaining why limitations were needed, the Register also stressed the implications that such a wider audience could have for the copyright owner:

Fully acknowledging the unique public value of educational broadcasting and its need for financial support, we must also recognize the large public audiences it is now reaching, the vast potential audiences that are awaiting it, and the fact that, as a medium for entertainment, recreation, and communication of information, a good deal of educational programming is indistinguishable from a good deal of commercial programming. In terms of good education, it is certainly true that the more people reached the better; but in terms of the author's rights it is equally true that the more people reached the more he should be compensated. It does not seem too much to ask that some of the money now going to support educational broadcasting activities be used to compensate authors and publishers whose works are essential to those activities.

As written, section 110(2) has only limited application to courses offered over a digital network. Taking the exemption out of the original context of analog broadcasting in the 1970s, and placing it in the digital distance education world of the late 1990s, raises a number of questions. While in 1976 the two section 110 exemptions were sufficient to cover "all of the various methods by which performances or displays in the course of systematic instruction take place," this may not be the case today, given the computer network technologies used in distance education programs.

A threshold question is whether the term "transmission" used in section 110(2) includes digital transmissions. The section itself does not specify any particular technology. To "transmit" a performance or display is defined in section 101 of the Copyright Act as "to communicate it by any device or process whereby images or sounds are received beyond the place from which they are sent." Since the definition is explicitly technology neutral ("any device or process"), digital transmissions should be covered. This conclusion does not resolve the matter, however. The problem is that most digital distance education is transmitted via computer networks. Section 110(2) does not effectively exempt these transmissions, as they implicate copyright rights other than the rights of performance and display. As discussed above, such digital transmission by definition involves multiple acts of reproduction, and often distribution, which are not covered by section 110(2). Therefore, even if the performance and display were exempted, these digital transmissions would result in an infringement unless the accompanying acts of reproduction and distribution were otherwise authorized.

Not all digital delivery methods would cause this problem. As discussed above, digital broadcasts that do not implicate rights beyond performance and display, and otherwise conform to the requirements of section 110(2), would be covered. An additional question is raised by the exemption's limitation on eligible recipients. At least in part because of the changes in transmission technologies, distance education has gained in appeal to a wider audience, and some of the new students may not fall within the scope of the exemption. Modern distance education programs could be considered the latter-day parallel of the "instructional television college credit courses" that, in the 1970s, were "fast becoming a valuable adjunct of the normal college curriculum." Students taking distance classes because of daytime employment, geographic remoteness, child care, or similar reasons, would likely qualify as persons whose "special circumstances prevent their attendance in classrooms." Students who choose to take a distance course for simple convenience or preference, or as a supplement to classroom courses, may not have the type of "intervening reason" contemplated by section 110(2), and so may not qualify as recipients.

Fair use is the broadest and most general limitation on the exclusive rights of copyright owners. It operates independently of the other exemptions in the Act, and can therefore exempt distance education uses not covered by sections 110(1) and 110(2). Codified in section 107, fair use is a flexible, technology-neutral doctrine, allowing reasonable and socially desirable uses of copyright works, even when they are not authorized by the copyright owner.

(a) *Application to education in general.* Fair use can apply to all types of uses, including educational uses. It is one of the exemptions intended to benefit education, with teaching, scholarship and research among the examples of fair use purposes cited in the statutory language. Section 107 begins by stating: Notwithstanding the provisions of sections 106 and 106A, the fair use of a copyrighted work, including such use by reproduction in copies or phonorecords or by any other means specified by that section, for purposes such as criticism, comment, news reporting, teaching (including multiple copies for classroom use), scholarship, or research, is not an infringement of copyright.The provision sets out four nonexclusive factors that a court must weigh in making a determination of whether any particular use is fair. The four statutory factors are:

(1) the purpose and character of the use, including whether such use is of a commercial nature or is for nonprofit educational purposes;

(2) the nature of the copyrighted work;

(3) the amount and substantiality of the portion used in relation to the copyrighted work as a whole; and

(4) the effect of the use upon the potential market for or value of the copyrighted work.The Supreme Court has made clear that there can be no bright line test for fair use, but that it must be adjudicated on a case-

by-case basis. The fact-based nature of the balancing test can make it difficult for a user to predict outcomes. Although many educational uses may qualify as fair use, others may not.

(b) *Application to digital distance education*. The legislative history to section 107 explicitly noted the potential application of fair use to distance education:

The fair use doctrine would be relevant to the use of excerpts from copyrighted works in educational broadcasting activities not exempted under section 110(2) or 112, and not covered by the licensing provisions of section 118. In these cases the factors to be weighed in applying the criteria of this section would include whether the performers, producers, directors, and others responsible for the broadcast were paid, the size and nature of the audience, the size and number of excerpts taken and, in the case of recordings made for broadcast, the number of copies reproduced and the extent of their reuse or exchange. The availability of the fair use doctrine to educational broadcasters would be narrowly circumscribed in the case of motion pictures and other audiovisual works, but under appropriate circumstances it could apply to the nonsequential showing of an individual still or slide, or to the performance of a short excerpt from a motion picture for criticism or comment.Fair use continues to be a critical exemption in the digital distance education context.

It has been the broadest and most flexible exemption for educational users in the analog world, and will continue this role in the digital world. The question is not whether fair use applies to distance education in a digital environment, but how it does. While there are not yet any cases addressing this issue, a court's analysis will depend on elements such as the subject matter of the course, the nature of the educational institution, the ways in which instructors use materials, and the kinds and amounts of materials used.

The first statutory factor, the purpose and character of the use, encompasses several variables. The first sentence of section 107 cites teaching, scholarship and research as examples of fair use purposes. To the extent that the use is for "nonprofit educational purposes," as specified in the first factor, it is more likely to be fair. In addition, uses that are "transformative," as opposed to merely reproductive or "consumptive," are favored. A transformative use is one that uses the copyrighted work as raw material from which to produce insight or understanding, generally expressed in a new creative work. Education often involves such transformative uses, although it does not always do so.

The second factor is the nature of the copyrighted work. In weighing this factor, courts generally look to whether the work is creative or factual, and whether it is unpublished or published. Creative works are considered "closer to the core of intended copyright protection" than factual works, and therefore are less subject to fair use. Whether a work used in the course of digital distance education is more factual or creative is likely to vary with the subject matter of the course. For example, a chemistry course is likely to use factual material, while a writing course is likely to focus on creative works.

Unpublished works are less subject to fair use than published ones because of the impact on the author's right to control the "first public appearance of his undisseminated expression." This aspect of the second factor is unpredictable in its application to distance education uses. Educators are likely to rely largely on published, available works to teach their classes. On the other hand, the curricula of certain types of classes, like graduate history courses, may incorporate unpublished materials such as letters or diaries.

Several other elements may be relevant to evaluation of the second fair use factor. In the educational context, a court may look at the intended audience for the copyrighted work itself. If it is a work prepared primarily for school markets, such as a textbook, "the defense of fair use would be far less appropriate than if the work were material prepared for the general public." The work's commercial availability might also be considered. A user may have more justification for using a work without permission if it is "unavailable for purchase through normal channels." These aspects of the nature of the work may also be relevant to the analysis of the other factors, particularly the impact of the use on the market for or value of the work.

The third fair use factor is the amount and substantiality of the portion used. The amounts of the portions of works used in an educational context will vary according to the teaching style of the instructor, the type of work, and the subject of the course. In some instances only excerpts of works may be used, such as in a survey course of English literature. In other cases the nature of the works being studied, such as short poems or paintings, will make it more likely that the whole work will be used. Because "the extent of permissible copying varies with the purpose and character of the use," the evaluation of the amount used will relate to the first factor as well.

The fourth factor, the effect of the use upon the potential market for or value of the work, in effect weighs the extent of the market harm caused by the user's conduct. The market to be considered includes not only opportunities for sale or license of the work itself, but also opportunities to license the creation of derivative works. This factor too will weigh differently for different distance education uses, and is intertwined with the analysis of the other three factors.

The purpose of the use, the nature of the work, and the substantiality of the portion taken are all likely to bear on how much the market for or value of the work is affected. Certain categories of works may be more susceptible to harm than others, such as materials produced primarily for use in instruction, or audiovisual works intended for a wide public audience that overlaps with traditional student populations. On the other hand, to the extent that a class is shown only a short excerpt of a work, the impact on the market is likely to be reduced.

In addition, the extent to which licenses are available for the work may play into the fair use balancing. The easy availability of a convenient mechanism for securing licenses at a reasonable cost, such as the Copyright Clearance Center, has been taken into account by the courts. As a corollary, the unavailability of an effective licensing mechanism could weigh in favor of a finding of fair use.In looking ,at digital distance education, characteristics specific to digital technologies are also likely to be relevant to the fourth factor.

Despite the fact that the fair use doctrine is technology-neutral, the way it applies to a particular use may be affected by the technology used. In particular, the ability in the digital environment to easily make and distribute vast numbers of perfect copies could alter a court's evaluation of this factor. Although this aspect of the technology increases the risk to the copyright owner's markets, there are potentially countervailing elements as well. For example, the deployment of technological measures that control access to works, or control their downstream uses, may also be considered.

Fair use guidelines. Several attempts have been made to provide greater certainty for both educational users and copyright owners under section 107, by crafting guidelines as to how fair use applies to educational uses. Guidelines are detailed standards describing permissible uses that represent a negotiated consensus among groups of interested parties. They do not have the force of law, do not control or alter statutory language, and are not binding on any party. Their purpose is to establish a "safe harbor" of conduct-a minimum standard that those endorsing them agree would qualify as fair use. They typically include guidance as to specific amounts of works that can safely be used for a particular purpose, the numbers of copies that can be made, and time periods for various uses. Operating within such guidelines substantially reduces the risk of suit.

Accordingly, they are helpful to educators in planning their conduct. It is important to stress, however, that they are a floor and not a ceiling; conduct that falls outside the guidelines may qualify as fair use as well. Despite the lack of legal force, courts have considered the contents of guidelines in evaluating fair use claims, and some have ruled in accordance with their principles. During the drafting of the 1976 Act, and immediately following its enactment, guidelines were negotiated to address several types of educational use: analog classroom photocopying, educational uses of music, and off-air taping of broadcast programs for educational purposes.

The legislative history of section 107 reproduces the guidelines for classroom photocopying and educational uses of music. The effort to draft off-air taping guidelines began in 1977 and the guidelines were finalized in 1981. All of these educational guidelines have been endorsed by a number of entities, with many endorsers expressing the view that they increase certainty and security.

Congress encouraged the interested parties to "continue their efforts to provide additional specific guidelines" in the future in "areas where standards other than [the photocopying and music] guidelines may be appropriate." After 1981, however, there were no efforts to draft fair use guidelines until the CONFU and CCUMC processes began in 1994, addressing the application of fair use in the digital environment.

Other exemptions in the Copyright Act may exempt certain distance education uses in limited circumstances, supplementing the exemptions discussed in the preceding section. While these additional exemptions are important to a full understanding of how the Copyright Act applies to education, they are unlikely to significantly expand the scope of permitted instructional uses in a digital environment.

(a) Section 112 - Ephemeral recordings. Section 112 permits the making of ephemeral recordings of transmission programs embodying the performance or display of copyrighted works in certain circumstances, for use in making transmissions that are authorized under various other provisions of the Act. This section was based upon "the traditional concept of ephemeral recordings as mere technical adjuncts of broadcasting that have no appreciable effect on the copyright owner's rights or market for the copies or phonorecords." Subsection (a) permits any transmitting organization to make a single copy of its authorized broadcasts under limited circumstances.

It responds to arguments by broadcasters that they needed to make limited reproductions for internal use to facilitate their broadcasts, and is intended to allow for the "practical exigencies of broadcasting." Subsection (b) permits governmental or nonprofit organizations entitled to transmit displays or performances under section 110(2) or 114(a) to make not more than thirty copies of a transmission program embodying the performance or display, and to retain the copies for not more than seven years (other than a single archival copy). No further copies may be made from these copies. The exemption operates as an adjunct to the exemptions for performance and display under sections 110(2) and 114(a), allowing a nonprofit educational institution to make certain reproductions to facilitate the permitted performance or display without having to seek a separate license to do so. It is available only to the transmitting organization, and would not permit the making of copies by students. This provision responds to arguments by educational organizations that recording instructional broadcasts was essential to their utility, since the same class would often be repeated asynchronously throughout the school day or over the years. In describing an earlier draft of section 112, the House Judiciary Committee noted that it was "aware of the practical problems facing educational broadcasters and other transmitters if they are required to seek separate clearances of performing and recording rights.

Section 112(b) has only limited applicability to digital distance education transmissions. It would permit, for example, the reproduction, and retention for seven years, of thirty copies of a digital broadcast of a transmission program authorized by section 110(2). It would also permit the making of archival copies of transmission programs involved in a course, provided that no further copies were made of the archival copies. However, it would not authorize the making of the transient reproductions necessary to the technical process of transmission in online courses for two reasons. First, it would be impossible, as a practical matter, to limit to thirty the RAM copies generated in the course of the transmission. Second, such copies inevitably generate further copies along the network, disqualifying the transmitting organization from the benefits of the exemption.

(b) Section 114 - Scope of exclusive rights in sound recordings. Until 1996, there was no performance right for sound recordings under U.S. copyright law. The Digital Performance Right in Sound Recordings Act of 1995 ("DPRA") amended section 106 of the Copyright Act to give owners of sound recordings the exclusive right "to perform the copyrighted work publicly by means of a digital audio transmission." The DPRA also amended section 114, which limits the scope of exclusive rights in sound recordings, and additional amendments were subsequently made in 1998 by the DMCA. In its current form, section 114 divides the types of transmissions that carry performances of sound recordings into three categories. Depending on the category into which the digital audio transmission falls, the performance of the sound recording could be subject to no right at all, a statutory license, or a full exclusive right.

The three categories of transmissions in section 114(d) are:

(1) nonsubscription broadcast transmissions (and certain retransmissions), which are completely exempted from the section 106(6) performance right;

(2) subscription transmissions and certain "eligible nonsubscription transmissions" such as webcasting, which are eligible for a statutory license, subject to a list of criteria; and

(3) interactive (on-demand) transmissions and other non-exempt transmissions that do not qualify for the statutory license, which are subject to the full exclusive performance right. All of these terms are defined at length in the statute.

The application of this complex structure to digital distance education will vary depending on the nature of the activity involved. Distance education activities that entail digital "broadcast transmissions" of sound recordings will not be subject to the section 106(6) performance right. "Broadcast" transmissions are defined for this purpose as transmissions carried out by FCC-licensed radio or television stations. It is possible that some distance education activities will be eligible for a statutory license under section 114(d)(2). To qualify for a statutory license, a digital transmission must be either a subscription transmission or an "eligible nonsubscription transmission." Certain distance education activities could entail subscription transmissions (transmissions that are controlled and limited to particular recipients, and for which payment is required). Other activities, such as those carried out synchronously by means of streaming audio, could be considered eligible nonsubscription transmissions. For either a subscription or eligible nonsubscription transmission to qualify for the statutory license, however, it must be noninteractive and meet a series of criteria set out in section 114, including not publishing the titles of the sound recordings in advance and not transmitting too many selections from the same phonorecord or by the same performer.Any digital transmission of a sound recording that is not exempt, and fails to meet all of the criteria to be eligible for the statutory license, will be subject to the full exclusive right under section 106(6). Because many asynchronous distance education activities are interactive, they will likely fall into this category.

Another paragraph of section 114 may also have some limited application to digital distance education uses. Section 114(b) limits the exclusive rights of reproduction, distribution and preparation of derivative works, so as not to apply to sound recordings included in "educational television and radio programs" distributed or transmitted by or through "public broadcasting entities," as those terms are defined by law, provided that copies are not commercially distributed to the general public. In an analog world this would mean that, in these circumstances, a sound recording could be performed, and the performance could be transmitted, reproduced, and distributed, since there is no analog performance right for soundrecordings. In the digital world, however, the right to perform the work under section 106(6), not exempted by section 114(b), would still apply. Even if the performance was permitted under section 106(6), section 114(b) would not exempt uses by institutions other than public broadcasting entities, or uses in connection with instruction that do not qualify as "educational television or radio programs" within the meaning of the statute.

Section 111(a) exempts certain secondary transmissions of primary transmissions embodying a performance or display of a work. A secondary transmission is defined as "the further transmitting of a primary transmission simultaneously with the primary transmission," or nonsimultaneously by a cable system outside the United States. Paragraph (a)(2) exempts secondary transmissions "made solely for the purpose and under the conditions specified by clause (2) of section 110." This provision does not materially expand the exemptions for distance educators, but merely "make[s] clear that an instructional transmission within the scope of section 110(2) is exempt whether it is a 'primary transmission' or a 'secondary transmission.'" For U.S. educational institutions, it would authorize only simultaneous transmissions of transmissions that are permitted under section 110(2).

Distance educators could obtain authorization to use some works in limited ways through a compulsory license. A compulsory license is a license established by statute that permits particular uses of works upon compliance with prescribed procedures, rates and terms.

In addition to the section 114(d) compulsory license for certain transmissions of sound recordings discussed above, two other provisions may be relevant to educators. Section 115 establishes a compulsory license to make and distribute phonorecords of nondramatic musical works. Section 118(d) establishes a compulsory license for public broadcasting entities for certain uses of published nondramatic musical works, or pictorial, graphic and sculptural works, in the course of a transmission made by a noncommercial educational broadcast station, subject to the terms of any voluntary, industry-wide license agreement. There are a number of restrictions on the eligibility for these licenses. Because of their limited applicability, they are not likely to be much used by digital distance educators.

Educational institutions today often provide network access for their communities of faculty, staff and students. Section 512 of the US Copyright Act, enacted as Title II of the DMCA, provides greater security that, merely by doing so, they will not become liable for infringing material transmitted over the network. This section limits the liability of online service providers for copyright infringement while engaging in certain types of activities. When the service providers, including educational institutions, meet the statutory criteria, they will not be held liable for damages.

In the course of providing digital distance education, an educational institution may act as a service provider rather than the originator of the transmission, and therefore be entitled to the benefit of section 512's limitations on liability. The limitations apply to four types of activity by a service provider:

1) transitory communications;

2) system caching;

3) storage of information on systems or networks at the direction of users; and

4) information location tools.

Each limitation entails a complete bar on monetary damages, and restricts the availability of injunctive relief in various respects.

In addition to detailed conditions contained in each of the four limitations, a service provider must meet two overall conditions:

(1) it must adopt and reasonably implement a policy of terminating in appropriate circumstances the accounts of subscribers who are repeat infringers; and

(2) it must accommodate and not interfere with standard technical measures used to protect and identify works. Section 512(e) provides special rules tailored to nonprofit educational institutions. It determines when the actions or knowledge of a faculty member or graduate student employee who is performing a teaching or research function may affect the eligibility of a nonprofit educational institution for the limitations on liability. In general, such a faculty member or graduate student shall be considered a separate person from the institution for purposes of determining who initiated the transmission, and his knowledge or awareness of infringement will not be attributed to the institution. For an institution to benefit from these rules, the following conditions must be met:

— the faculty member or graduate student's infringing activities do not involve providing online access to course materials that were required or recommended during the past three years;

— the institution has not received more than two notifications over the past three years that the faculty member or graduate student was infringing; and

— the institution provides all of its users with informational materials describing and promoting compliance with copyright law.

Section 512 will not affect an educational institution's legal obligations as a provider of content. When an educator selects material to be used in teaching a course, and determines how it will be used and to whom it will be transmitted, he is subject to the standard copyright rules described above.

The DMCA also added a new Chapter 12 to Title 17 of the U.S. Code, providing technological adjuncts to copyright protection in order to make digital networks safe for the exploitation and licensing of copyrighted works. These provisions should assist in lessening some of the risks involved in digital distance education. Section 1201 of this Chapter contains a prohibition against the circumvention of technological measures used by copyright owners to protect their works. Section 1202 protects the integrity of copyright management information ("CMI") that may accompany a copyrighted work, ensuring that the public is able to rely on such information.

Section 1201 divides technological measures into two categories: measures that prevent unauthorized access to a copyrighted work, and measures that prevent unauthorized copying. As to either type of measure, the section makes it illegal to make or sell devices or services that are used to circumvent, in specified circumstances. As to access control measures only, the act of circumvention in itself is also subject to a prohibition. While violations may give rise to both civil and criminal penalties, nonprofit libraries, archives and educational institutions are entitled to a complete remission of damages in civil cases if the violation was innocent, and are entirely exempted from criminal liability.

The prohibition on the act of circumventing access controls does not take effect, however, until two years after the statute's enactment. It is subject to an exception for users of a work in a particular class of works who are likely to be adversely affected by the prohibition in their ability to make noninfringing uses.

The applicability of the exception will be determined though a periodic rulemaking by the Librarian of Congress on the recommendation of the Register of Copyrights, after consultation with the Assistant Secretary of Commerce for Communications and Information. Those digital distance education uses that are exempted from liability in the Copyright Act, now or in the future, could be among the noninfringing uses taken into account in the rulemaking.

Section 1202 makes it illegal deliberately to remove or alter CMI, or to provide false CMI with the intent to assist infringement. CMI is defined as identifying information about the work, the author, the copyright owner, and in certain cases, the performer, writer or director, as well as terms and conditions for use of the work, and such other information as the Register of Copyrights may prescribe by regulation.

These provisions do not affect the existence or scope of digital distance education exemptions, or determine whether a particular use is infringing. They are relevant to distance education, however, in that they should strengthen the ability of both educators and copyright owners to effectively protect the security of transmitted material in a digital environment.

By protecting against the circumvention of technological measures, and safeguarding the integrity of information which can be used to locate owners, license educational uses of digital materials, and identify infringing copies, these provisions can help to facilitate licensing and reduce the risks of unauthorized access and use.

The United States is a party to a number of treaties which impose obligations with respect to copyright. Any change to the copyright law of the United States must take into account these international obligations. The two major multilateral treaties dealing with copyright are the Berne Convention for the Protection of Literary and Artistic Works ("Berne") and the World Trade Organization ("WTO") Agreement on the Trade-Related Aspects of Intellectual Property Rights (1994) ("TRIPs"). These treaties require member countries to provide certain minimum copyright rights, and limit the scope of permissible exceptions to those rights.

The Berne Convention establishes the basic foundation upon which most other copyright-related treaties are built. Berne requires member countries to grant to authors certain exclusive rights, including rights of reproduction, public performance, broadcasting and other means of communication to the public, and adaptation. Different rules govern the permissibility of exceptions to different rights. Some Berne exceptions are applicable to all rights. Most relevant here is article 10(2), which allows members to adopt legislation "to permit the utilization, to the extent justified by the purpose, of literary or artistic works by way of illustration in publications, broadcasts or sound or visual recordings for teaching, provided such utilization is compatible with fair practice."

As to the reproduction right, article 9(2) provides that exceptions are permitted in "certain special cases, provided that such reproduction does not conflict with a normal exploitation of the work and does not unreasonably prejudice the legitimate interests of the author."

Other rights are subject to certain specific exceptions, supplemented by the "minor exceptions" generally agreed to be permitted by implication, provided that they are de minimis.The TRIPs Agreement incorporates the substantive obligations of Berne, and goes beyond them in various respects. In particular, the limits on exceptions to the reproduction right established in Berne article 9(2) are extended to apply to exceptions to all exclusive rights. Article 13 of TRIPs states:

> Members shall confine limitations or exceptions to exclusive rights to certain special cases which do not conflict with a normal exploitation of the work and do not unreasonably prejudice the legitimate interests of the right holder.

Berne and TRIPs have recently been updated and supplemented by two new treaties concluded at the World Intellectual Property Organization ("WIPO") in 1996: the WIPO Copyright Treaty ("WCT") and the WIPO Performances and Phonograms Treaty ("WPPT") (together "WIPO Treaties"). These treaties, which are not yet in force, contain provisions to ensure that the balance of rights between copyright owners and users will be carried forward into the digital age. They include certain additional rights for copyright owners, and extend the Berne article 9(2) standard to all of these new rights, as well as to all rights in Berne. Both treaties contain identical Agreed Statements explicating the application of this traditional standard in the digital environment:

> It is understood that the provisions of [this] Article . . . permit Contracting Parties to carry forward and appropriately extend into the digital environment limitations and exceptions in their national laws which have been considered acceptable under the Berne Convention. Similarly, these provisions should be understood to permit Contracting Parties to devise new exceptions and limitations that are appropriate in the digital network environment. It is also understood that [this] Article . . . neither reduces nor extends the scope of applicability of the limitations and exceptions permitted by the Berne Convention. This language represents the consensus of the more than 100 countries that participated in the negotiations as to the interpretation of Berne article 9(2).

Any new or amended exemption for distance education should be drafted to be compatible with the standards of TRIPs article 13 and Berne article 9(2). Such an exemption should be confined to "certain special cases," and neither conflict with normal exploitation of the work, nor unreasonably prejudice the copyright owner. Under article 10(2), a use "by way of illustration . . . for teaching" may be permitted "to the extent justified by the purpose," if "compatible with fair practice." Whether any particular exemption would satisfy these standards will depend on its scope and effect. The broader the exemption, the more likely that our trading partners might claim that it was inconsistent with Berne and TRIPs obligations.

An additional issue in the international arena is the effect that any new exemption for digital distance education might have abroad. When educational institutions in the United States transmit courses to students in other countries, a number of legal questions are raised, relating to choice of law. Which country's law determines the ownership of the course materials (either the course itself or the preexisting materials it contains)? Which country's law determines whether particular license terms are valid, and how they should be interpreted? Which country's law determines the scope of the copyright owner's rights, and whether the acts of the educational institution constitute an infringement? If a lawsuit is brought, there may be additional procedural questions of jurisdiction, venue, and enforcement of judgments.

Under existing legal doctrines, the answers to these questions are far from clear. In the traditional analog world, the majority view has been that questions of authorship and ownership are determined by the law of the work's country of origin. The validity and meaning of a contract is generally determined by the law of the country with the most significant connections to the contract. The scope of rights, and therefore what acts constitute infringements, is determined by the law of the country where the acts took place. The latter rule is based on the principle of territoriality, under which each country grants a national copyright, and defines the nature and scope of the rights that are enjoyed within its own borders. The problem is that in the digital environment, it becomes less clear where the relevant act took place. In the case of a digital transmission, is it the country where the transmitting organization resides, where the server is located, where the student is enrolled, or where the transmission is received by the student? Various proposals have been suggested, but there are no definitive answers. It is therefore hard to predict whether any new exemption in U.S. law might be applied to the transmission of a distance education program by an American university to a student in another country.

If the law of the country where the transmission is received is found to apply, universities will have difficulty determining what conduct is permissible, especially if courses are transmitted to students in many countries. The content of other countries' laws on distance education will become increasingly important to U.S. educators. It should be kept in mind, however, that because most countries today are party to the Berne Convention or the TRIPs Agreement, their laws should comply with the restrictions described above.

Although it was not possible in the time allotted to this study to research thoroughly the laws of other countries, we understand that several are considering amendments to their copyright laws to deal with digital distance education issues. Their general approach is to update existing statutory or collective licensing provisions on educational photocopying and/or off-air taping to include digital reproduction by educational institutions. It is not clear what types of digital reproductions would be covered or whether other rights might be included. To our knowledge, the only country that has to date enacted such legislation is Denmark, although Canada and Australia are reportedly considering similar changes.

The European Union is considering a directive that would harmonize its member states' laws in this area. The proposed Directive on the Harmonization of Certain Aspects of Copyright and Related Rights in the Information Society, in the version currently being considered by the European Commission, would allow member states to establish limitations on the rights of reproduction and communication to the public permitting a single use for the purpose of illustration for teaching, as long as the source is indicated and to the extent justified by the noncommercial purpose, on the condition that the rights holder receives equitable compensation.

The first in-depth public discussion of the issue of copyright law and digital distance education began nearly five years ago, in the context of an examination of how the fair use doctrine applies in the digital environment. Two different initiatives in this area began separately and proceeded on parallel tracks, with varying results. Both sought to develop guidelines interpreting the parameters of fair use in connection with certain educational uses of copyrighted works through digital technology.One working group was begun in June 1994, at the instigation of the Consortium of College and University Media Centers ("CCUMC") and the Agency for Instructional Technology (AIT), to examine the possibility of drafting fair use guidelines for educational multimedia. The second was an outgrowth of the Conference on Fair Use ("CONFU") convened in September 1994 by the Working Group on Intellectual Property Rights of the Clinton Administration's Information Infrastructure Task Force, chaired by the Commissioner of Patents and Trademarks. CONFU established a number of working groups on different topics, including one on distance learning.

Both the CCUMC group and the CONFU Working Group on Distance Learning engaged in intensive debate of the issues over a period of several years. Each included a wide range of interested parties from the educational, library, and copyright owner communities, with different participants active in the process at different points. While the two groups addressed different subjects, they shared numerous participants and kept abreast of each other's activities.

A greater mutual understanding of the issues, with considerable agreement developed as to which activities should or should not be permissible. Both groups were also successful in preparing draft guidelines, one dealing with the use of copyrighted works in educational multimedia projects created by educators or students, and the other dealing with the performance and display of copyrighted works in distance learning classes. Ultimately, the entire process became controversial, both because of conflicting views of the value and function of fair use guidelines generally, and due to anticipation of possible Congressional action, including on the subject of distance education. As a result, none of the guidelines were formally adopted by CONFU.

Nevertheless, the educational multimedia and distance learning guidelines have had an impact on the world of education. A number of organizations and companies have officially endorsed them or unofficially rely on them for guidance. These earlier efforts are of interest here in several respects. They are not directly relevant as a point of comparison, since the Copyright Office study is not limited to an examination of fair use, but focuses on proposed changes to section 110(2).

After two years of negotiation, the working group coordinated by the CCUMC issued a set of guidelines on educational multimedia in September 1996, and proceeded with its own process for review and endorsement. The guidelines were published in a non-legislative report of the House of Representatives Subcommittee on Courts and Intellectual Property, described as "an agreed upon interpretation of the fair use provisions of the Copyright Act by the overwhelming majority of institutions and organization affected by educational multimedia." CONFU also subsequently adopted the Fair Use Guidelines for Educational Multimedia as a CONFU proposal.

Although maintained as a parallel initiative by CCUMC, these guidelines are also regarded as a product of the CONFU process. The guidelines provide guidance for "the fair use of portions of lawfully acquired copyrighted works in educational multimedia projects which are created by educators or students as part of a systematic learning activity at nonprofit educational institutions." The guidelines cover students producing such projects for a specific course, and educators doing so "for their own teaching tools in support of curriculum-based instructional activities at educational institutions." They set out specific criteria for the length of time the projects may be used, the portions of different types of copyrighted works that may be used, and the copying and distribution of the projects. They also state that students "should be instructed about the reasons for copyright protection and the need to follow these guidelines," remind both educators and students to provide attribution and acknowledgments, and advise them that they must include a notice of use restrictions under copyright law on the opening screen of the program and any accompanying print material.

Although the preamble states that the guidelines "are not intended to cover fair use of copyrighted works in other educational contexts such as . . . distance education, or electronic reserves," they do provide guidance for certain uses within a general definition of distance education. The guidelines state that educators may perform and display their own educational multimedia projects "for remote instruction to students enrolled in curriculum-based courses and located at remote sites provided over the educational institution's secure electronic network in real-time . . . ." They further allow for limited delayed or asynchronous use: If the educational institution's network or technology used to access the educational multimedia project created under Section 2 of these guidelines cannot prevent duplication of copyrighted material, students or educators may use the multimedia educational projects over an otherwise secure network for a period of only 15 days after its initial real-time remote use in the course of instruction or 15 days after its assignment for directed self-study.

The Educational Multimedia Fair Use Guidelines have been endorsed by numerous associations representing educational institutions, licensing organizations and content providers, as well as individual companies, and support for them has been expressed by some governmental agencies. In CONFU, because there was substantial support but no general consensus among participants, it was suggested that the guidelines be tried and monitored for two or three years. Many educational institutions across the country at both the K-12 and post-secondary levels are using them as a reference or link to them on their websites.

The CONFU Distance Learning Working Group submitted its draft guidelines as a proposal in November 1996, explaining:

> The purpose of these guidelines is to provide guidance for the performance and display of copyrighted works in some of the distance learning environments that have developed since the enactment of Section 110 and that may not meet the specific conditions of Section 110(2). They permit instructors who meet the conditions of these

guidelines to perform and display copyrighted works as if they were engaged in face-to-face instruction.The proposed guidelines apply to the performance and display of lawfully acquired copyrighted works, such as dramatic or audiovisual works, that are not included under section 110(2), as well as to types of uses that are not addressed in that section.

The guidelines address the following uses: "(1) live interactive distance learning classes (i.e., a teacher in a live class with all or some of the students at remote locations) and (2) faculty instruction recorded without students present for later transmission. They apply to delivery via satellite, closed circuit television or secure computer network." Although the guidelines interpret the fair use doctrine, they are explicitly informed by the principles of section 110(2), and adopt a number of its concepts. The guidelines similarly apply only to nonprofit educational institutions, but add the limitation that the use must also be noncommercial. The students who may view the transmission must be officially enrolled in the course. Unlike section 110(2), the guidelines would permit the use of any category of copyrighted work.

The acts described above are considered to fall within the guidelines only if various restrictions are met: First, the works performed must be "integrated into the course," as well as meeting requirements similar to those in section 110(2) of being part of systematic instruction, and directly related and of material assistance to the teaching content of the transmission. The performance may not be for entertainment purposes. Second, technological measures must be used to prevent unauthorized access or copying, and the transmission must be received in a classroom or other location where the reception can be controlled by the institution. Finally, while there is no limit on the amounts of works that can be used, if an entire work or a large portion thereof is performed, it may be transmitted only once without obtaining permission.

Although the working group discussed distance learning generally, the draft guidelines focused primarily on synchronous delivery. Some participants believed that the time was not ripe for consideration of asynchronous delivery over a computer network. They explained that "the technology is rapidly developing, educational institutions are only now beginning to experiment with such distance learning courses, and publishers and other content creators are in the early stages of developing materials and marketing strategies for publisher-produced computer network delivery of distance learning materials."

Other participants, primarily educational representatives managing network-based distance learning programs or assisting with their support, believed that guidelines for distance learning that failed to cover asynchronous delivery would not adequately address the concerns of the educational community. Given this lack of consensus and the limited time available, the proposed guidelines "do not cover asynchronous delivery of distance learning over a computer network, even one that is secure and capable of limiting access to students enrolled in the course through PIN or other identification system."The proposed guidelines, like the Educational Multimedia Guidelines, do address certain asynchronous uses. Under the guidelines, an eligible institution "may record or copy classes that include the performance of an entire copyrighted work, or a large portion thereof, and retain the recorded copy for up to 15 consecutive class days (i.e., days in which the institution is open for regular instruction) for viewing by students enrolled in the course." Permission is required, however, for further dissemination of recorded courses.

While many organizations had endorsed the proposed guidelines, a significant number of CONFU participants were dissatisfied. Among the sources of dissatisfaction was the failure to address asynchronous computer network delivery. The Distance Learning Working Group was expanded by inviting additional representatives from the educational community, with the goal of developing guidelines for asynchronous computer network delivery of distance learning courses. The reconstituted group met twice in the fall of 1997, but its discussions came to an end without conclusion in the midst of the controversy about the advisability of guidelines in general.

The CONFU proposed distance learning guidelines have been endorsed by a number of entities, including library and educational associations and content owners, and some institutions are using them as a reference or linking to them.

In 1997, two bills were introduced in US House and Senate, each proposing a number of amendments to the Copyright Act to address issues raised by digital technologies. One of 120 the proposed amendments in both bills dealt with the distance education exemption in section 110(2).

The bills would have amended section 110(2) to exempt:performance, display or distribution of a work, by or in the course of an analog or digital transmission, if-

(A) the performance, display or distribution is a regular part of the systematic instructional activities of a governmental body or a nonprofit educational institution;

(B) the performance, display or distribution is directly related and of material assistance to the teaching content of the transmission; and

(C) the work is provided for reception by-

(i) students officially enrolled in the course in connection with which it is provided; or

(ii) officers or employees of governmental bodies as part of their official duties or employment, . . . Thus, the amendment would have clarified that the exempted transmission could be analog or digital. It would also have broadened the scope of the exemption by enlarging upon the works, the rights, and the locations covered. First, the categories of works would have been expanded, removing the existing limitation to a "nondramatic literary or musical work" and allowing performance of any type of work. Second, while the current Act exempts only the exercise of the rights of performance and display, the amendment would have added the right of distribution. Third, the amendment would have expanded the permissible locations to which the transmission could be made, removing the limitation that the transmission be made primarily for reception in classrooms and by people prevented from classroom attendance by.121 disabilities or other special circumstances, and allowing transmissions for reception by any student officially enrolled in the course.

The limits established by paragraphs (A) and (B) of existing section 110(2), however, would have remained. To qualify for the exemption, any transmitted work would still have had to be conveyed as part of the "systematic instructional activities of a governmental body or nonprofit educational institution," and be "directly related and of material assistance to the teaching content of the transmission." No floor action was taken on these bills.

In 1997, the Senate took up consideration of the World Intellectual Property Organization Copyright and Performances and Phonograms Treaty Implementation Act of 1997. During discussions in the Committee on the Judiciary, the subject of digital distance education was raised.

In the spring of 1998, Senators Orrin G. Hatch, Patrick J. Leahy and John Ashcroft brought together various interested parties to determine whether an agreement could be reached on an amendment for distance education. When the parties were unable to reach agreement, Senators Hatch, Leahy and Ashcroft requested that the Copyright Office facilitate further negotiations on the subject and make recommendations within several days, including legislative language if possible.

The distance education negotiations facilitated by the Copyright Office took place on April 27-28, 1998. They were presided over by the Register of Copyrights and involved representatives and associations of copyright owners, licensing organizations, educational institutions, and libraries and archives. Numerous issues were addressed, including the threshold question of whether or not the law should be changed to address the use of copyrighted works in digital distance education. Subsidiary issues included what, if any, limitations should be imposed on the type and quantity of works used, which exclusive rights should be covered, who should be eligible for any exemption, and appropriate limitations on the recipients of transmissions and their location. The participants discussed at some length the availability, effectiveness, and need for technological measures to limit reception of copyrighted works to authorized recipients and prevent unauthorized downstream use. The implementation of institutional policies and training about copyright for students and faculty engaged in digital distance education was also discussed, as was the role of licensing. Finally, the possibility was raised of a study assessing the system after an appropriate period of time.

During this process, it became clear that many complex and interrelated issues were involved that could not be given adequate consideration in the limited time available. Nor could all stakeholders be identified and consulted.

On April 29, 1998, the Copyright Office submitted its initial recommendations to Senators Hatch, Leahy and Ashcroft. The recommendations included statutory language for a narrow amendment to section 110(2), and a proposal for a subsequent study of the broader issues involved in digital distance education.The amendment to section 110(2) was intended to update it to allow the same instructional broadcasting activities to take place using digital technologies. It would have permitted performance of a nondramatic literary or musical work or display of a work by or in the course of an analog or noninteractive digital transmission, and reproduction of such work in intermediate, transient copies made in the course of a digital transmission, if -

(A) the performance or display is a regular part of the systematic instructional activities of a governmental body or a nonprofit educational institution; and

(B) the performance or display is directly related and of material assistance to the teaching content of the transmission; and

(C) the transmission is made primarily for -

i) reception in classrooms or similar places normally devoted to instruction, or

ii) reception by persons to whom the transmission is directed because their disabilities or other special circumstances prevent their attendance in classrooms or similar places normally devoted to instruction, or

iii) reception by officers or employees of governmental bodies as a part of their official duties or employment; and

(D) any intermediate, transient copies made in the course of the transmission are retained for no longer than reasonably necessary to complete the transmission.

The Copyright Office also recommended adding the following definition of "noninteractive" digital transmission to section 101:

> A digital transmission is "noninteractive," for purposes of section 110(2), when the transmission is made -
>
> (1) through a communications medium that does not afford an opportunity for the recipient to communicate a response to the person making the transmission through that medium; and
>
> (2) at a time or times determined by the person making the transmission.

Given the compressed time frame, this recommendation was intended as a minimalist approach, seeking to update the exemption without broadening it. It would have retained all of the existing limitations, adding only language that appeared necessary as a technical matter to permit instructional broadcasting to be carried out using digital broadcast technologies.

Because interactive transmissions raised more complex issues and potentially greater risks, the amended section 110(2) would have covered only noninteractive transmissions, and not on-demand digital transmissions. The Copyright Office did not at that time suggest alterations to the categories of works or the recipients and locations covered by the exemption, or include provisions regarding the use of technological protection measures or the implementation of copyright policies. In the subsequent study, the Copyright Office proposed to address the extent to which a new exemption was appropriate for transmissions over the Internet, or for interactive or on-demand distance learning activities over digital networks generally. The Office further proposed to examine the extent to which additional categories of works should be covered, and whether the employment of technological protection measures in connection with digital transmissions of copyrighted works should be required as a condition of eligibility.

The legislative amendment recommended by the Copyright Office in 1998 was not supported by the parties involved in the discussions. Some believed it was too narrow, and some too broad. The Senate opted not to amend section 110(2) at that time, instead mandating a study by the Copyright Office of the overall subject of the promotion of distance education through digital technologies. Such a study was also incorporated into the version of the bill passed by the House, and ultimately became section 403 of the DMCA. All participants in the US Copyright Office process agree that digital distance education should be fostered and facilitated; all want the field to thrive. The disagreement centers on how best to achieve that result-in particular, whether existing copyright law is adequate or should be changed.

7

The Future of Distance Learning

The ability of the computer to structure the communication procedures and protocols around the educational application and the nature of the learners was leading us to a quantum improvement in the educational process. Improving the ability to hold direct communications with a much greater number of the class members and to encourage the equality of student discussion as well as the introduction of collaborative learning methods provides results that could not objectively be measured in the traditional exam and grading approaches.

The use of asynchronous communications for education and training has been popularized into the rapidly growing metaphor of Asynchronous Learning Networks (ALN), many of us have become more than a little upset at some of the misconceptions and misapplications beginning to occur with respect to applying computer networking to higher education. Historically it is no comfort that this is the process that often occurs when new ideas based upon visions become popularized and introduced with a limited understanding of the their roots. Furthermore the administrative practices, management, and policies currently associated with distance education are encouraging exactly the wrong approach to utilize the technology to improve learning and increase the quality of the educational delivery process. It is quite clear historically in the field of Management Information Systems that new information and computer system technologies can be misdirected if the underlying human organizations and customs are not adapted to make the best use of the technology.

In US, college tuition can range from approximately \$3,000 to \$30,000 for an academic year. Recently the concept of the average student being right out of high school has been overturned and the majority of college students have been, or are, in the work place. They are older, may have a family, and are possibly part time students. They do not get much financial aid and student loan programs are not anywhere as generous as previously. The result is that the college student is becoming more of a mature consumer who is serious about finding the college program that will produce the best possible outcome for what he or she can afford to invest.

Many distance students being attracted to the ALN programs are the more valuable employees who never considered that they could take the time needed for regular courses. At the graduate level students in technical fields seek companies for jobs that will pay for their courses on a part time basis. Clearly many of the current ALN programs have been designed to "skim the cream" of the crop that these students represent. Higher education in the U.S. does not have a very effective lobby and many state supported institutions are facing, at best, semi-static budgets that are in effect cuts that cause increased tuition. The true costs at most state institutions would result in a tuition $15,000 or more if the student had to pay full costs. Outstanding private institutions cost about $25,000 but are subsidized, in addition, by endowments.

Today, one could start a pure electronic virtual university for about 2000 students with a tuition of around $15,000, where every single faculty member was paid a flat $150,000 a year and class size would be in the 25-30 student range. The initial funding to get off the ground would be fifteen million dollars. This would also allow each accepted student to take some initial courses free of charge. This cost is less than a new building on most college campus in the United States. Clearly there are no colleges where all faculty get that salary but if it did, it would certainly attract a faculty of top educators. Today most institutions would rather spend that chunk of funds on a new building.

At many institutions distance education is a separate administrative operation from the academic departments. Furthermore, the administration of distance education and the responsibility for the delivery of the courses is often in the hands of the distance education administration and not under the faculty in the department that normally has the academic governance authority over the face-to-face courses and their content. A significant percentage of the courses in distance education, at a growing number of institutions, are taught by adjuncts and non faculty staff. Since the cost of such courses is usually lower, the administration comes to view such programs as a sources of a "profit" in the cash flow. The distance learning operation often works on a fixed fee and the remainder of the tuition paid by the student is returned to the general budget funds.

Properties of the force should include:

— The World Wide Web and the Internet make ALN's (anytime, any where) delivery of courses by computer networks a viable alternative for millions of students.

— As a result of costs, college students are becoming intelligent consumers.

— Costs of tuition are continuing to rise and no end is in sight.

— Public funds for higher education are decreasing on a relative basis.

— The typical college student is older, working, may have a family and will likely be a part time student.

— The typical student will consider distance courses a viable alternative and in some ways more effective for their efficient mastery of the material.

— No institution of higher education will have a geographical monopoly they can count on.

— Institutions in the US are viewing Distance Education as a magical source of money.

— Institutions are viewing distance education as a source for new students who are both talented and well to do.

— Administrators are after technology that will automate the delivery of material with a minimum of academic person power.

— Institutions offering similar programs will be in very direct competition even though they may be thousands of miles apart.

— Many students will have to rely on support from the companies they work for and the companies will want programs that improve the short term benefits of the student to the company.

Effect of Commercialization

Commercialization of the field of higher education is probably the most visible of the consequences of the force. There are companies in the U.S. that allow employees they fund for a higher education to sign up only for courses that they feel are consistent with their objectives for the employee. Most surveys of industry views and academic views of what is important subject matter, even in the technical fields, show significant differences of views. This difference is often associated with short and long term views of what is important. The common goal conflict is between learning fundamentals (e.g., the theoretical constructs for any computer language) as a basis for life long learning ability and training for specific current skills (e.g., a course in Java) desired in today's marketplace.

There is also a view by some universities administrators that if the courses are just put on the web with some programs to give exercises and some adjunct faculty, teaching staff, or student labor to run a hundred students per section, then thousands of students will flock to these "automated" courses and all the financial problems will go away. The U.S. has invested sizable capital into trying to establish local colleges so everyone had easy geographical access. These will probably be the first institutions to be hit hard by distance programs from major universities and from commercial sources of training.

Current trends seem to indicate that there is going to be a tremendous long term shakeout of marginal institutions that cannot deliver quality education or meaningful full degree programs. Today you can buy videos of "lectures of Harvard Professors" on the open market. We are entering a period of what may be intense competition and commercialism for higher education that will spread beyond national boundaries. The commercial training programs to aid students to prepare for the GREs, GMATs, and MCATs are indications of the future. Does the student perform on these examinations of college abilities because of their college education or because of the training programs for them?

There are a number of commercial companies that advertise that they will create a virtual university/college on the web for any institution. They will come to your college and in five days train the professors how to transfer their courses to the web, how to teach on the web, and they will manage the whole operation for you. It does not matter to them what subject you are talking about, they have a single approach that is suppose to work for any discipline and any degree program. They quote numbers such as, it will take a professor only thirty hours to convert his or her existing course to the web.

There is no awareness that the best way to teach by using the technology may be completely different than what is normally done in the physical face-to-face environment. There is no recognition of the need to rethink the education process and the associated methodologies. The growing number of these academic consultants and web based real-estate developers for the virtual campuses are evidence of the commercialization process that seems to be overtaking higher education.

Many companies are backing off from their sizable investment in internal training programs are turning back to colleges and universities to take up the slack. They find the idea of distance education attractive to reach their nationally and internationally spread workforce. However, they speak in terms of such concepts as "just in time training" like learning is analogous to an inventory system. They confuse learning and training and are pushing institutions to offer small chunks of education such as certificate programs that are also degree accredited. While there is a role for colleges and universities to deliver training, the traditional objective of higher education is to deliver a product to the "student" that is the "mastery" of the subject and allows him or her to advance their career even if that means giving the student the ability to get qualify for a new job in a different organization. Concepts of "just in time training" and training in current technologies, in limited packages, is an educational mission that serves the company and not the student. With industry picking up an increasing share of the costs of tuition for students they are beginning to influence the objectives of the educational mission and it may not always be in a direction beneficial to the interests of the student. This may be a more long term force of commercialization than the prior one but it is probably a more dangerous one.

While there are movements to try to do away with tenure in the educational system in the U.S., it is not the more obvious lobby efforts that are worrisome. What is of concern is the subtle administrative practices that can, over a long period of time, significantly reduce tenure as an important component of higher education and eliminate the safeguard it represents for the educational process. The more insidious approach is the hiring of full time "qualified" staff to do teaching and the necessary use of adjuncts. Young untenured faculty are hired in great number and they are encouraged to focus on research and seeking funds for research. They are alleviated from teaching many undergraduate courses and these are taken over by full time staff, regular adjuncts, and even "visiting" professors.

While the untenured faculty think this is fine, it is fundamental change in higher education objectives by decreasing the importance of faculty performance in education at the undergraduate level. What is not realized is that some of these untenured faculty are being groomed for those staff positions when it becomes clear they will not succeed to get tenure. What they are judged on is their ability to bring in research funding and generate publications. Of course the long term implication of this is that the tenure decision is no longer viewed as important or serious. If they don't succeed they can become staff. They will end up as contract research appointments or full time teaching staff. The condition to get tenure will become so stiff that only a negligible number will get through that filter. A few decades of this and the tenured faculty will be a true minority of those teaching and gradually fade away.

Today, a degree program in some technical fields formulated around advertised jargon in the marketplace rather than meaningful bodies of scientific and technical knowledge. It is like a degree in sociology would become a degree in the behavior of the X-generation because advertisement firms wish to hire people who can graduate and be prepared to immediately design adds for that market group. Industry is sometimes more interested in the student being certified in a particular software system then in obtaining an understanding of the fundamentals and theoretical principles that underlie all such systems.

Over the past few decades many institutions in the U.S. have gone from situations where the majority of the salaries at the institution were faculty salaries to a situation today where a majority of the salaries are in administration and non tenure lines for research and teaching staff, sometimes referred to as research faculty, adjunct faculty, and/or fellows. Fore example , The New Jersey Institute of Technology (NJIT, US) numbers are used here to illustrate some important quantitative results. Dividing the instructional salary ($26,262,000) by 300 faculty members, the average faculty salary of $87,540 that includes approximately 25% overhead and a normal teaching load of 6 courses a year and two units for research and administrative activities. Therefore, the faculty cost for a course is around $10,942 (1/8 of the $87,540). Ph.D. students all get involved in teaching a course, grading material, and/or running problem sections. Their compensation including tuition is about $15,000, for which they may be involved in teaching two courses or aiding in four by grading or conducting problem sessions. It is fair to consider this an average of three courses. So the average cost when a Ph.D. student teaches a course is $5,000. However, it is usually considered that learning to teach is part of a Ph.D. student's training and usually he or she would be mentored by the faculty member in charge of the course and be provided with the faculty member's notes and materials. Furthermore, in the VC environment (use of a conference system) the faculty member can actually "listen in" on what is happening and dynamically guide the student or step in when needed by reading the evolving conference. In principle the academic department is in charge of insuring the quality of the people doing this and it is certainly true there are a number of excellent industrial people and ex-students willing to do this for the experience and pleasure rather than the pay. However, there are still times when individuals are brought in who do inadequate jobs and fail to really accomplish the objectives of the course.

The administrative level is the wrong place to insure quality; that task has to be done by a faculty member who must have some degree of responsibility for the particular course and its content. In general, the pay scales are too low to insure that all adjuncts perform at the level of quality they should, and there is no incentive for faculty to mentor these adjuncts in the same manner that they would doctoral students. With all the emphasis on using adjuncts to save money one has to wonder why administrators have not discovered the concept of the "adjunct administrator." This could a retired executive or downsized manager hired on a part time basis to analyze and make specific management decisions. All the arguments made for use of adjunct faculty should apply equally well to saving the costs of management overhead through the use of adjunct administrators.

Currently many institutions provide faculty rights to course materials for the purpose of ownership of textbooks but they have introduced far more limited rights with respect to software and videotapes. The technology is moving quickly to the point where a book is going to become software (including programs, video, and sound material) and that is going to lead to much conflict since all these nice distinctions completely break down. The Collaborative Hypertext concept would lead to dynamic knowledge bases developed collaboratively by the students and the instructor and updated with each new offering of the course. It would completely replace, in the long run, the text book and each new course offering would provide a CD-ROM of the current state of the knowledge base. The sizable difference between adjunct pay and faculty pay is exactly what leads to associated labor - management problems and some mistrust of administrative intentions on the part of the faculty. It is an unhealthy long term motivation factor. All this might sound like a great economic opportunity to administrators. However, now that students will be able to select a single degree program from hundreds of offering Universities they will also be able to buy and will pay for impartial assessments of the quality of these alternatives. Independent evaluations of not only programs but specific instructors and courses will also become commercial commodities on the web . After all a year of college is like buying a car and one can now purchase evaluations of cars on the web.

The use of adjuncts is actually an important slack resource that needs to be employed to allow for swings in load requirements that can occur because of short term research commitments. Furthermore there is justification for some number of full time teaching staff to handle the training missions of the universities. However, adjuncts and teaching staff should be under the direct supervision of the faculty in charge of a course and they should be reviewed by the appropriate faculty committees to be qualified for the courses they teach. In many situations such as separate distance learning programs this is not the case. In some institutions there is no uniform policy on the supervision of adjuncts or full time teaching staff and it is resolved on a department by department basis.

The office of Distance Learning at NJIT receives one fee for each true remote student and a much lesser fee for each on campus student who takes a distance learning course. The on campus student taking a distance course needs the same exact services from the distance learning office as the true remote student. They have an unsolved problem in providing the resources to handle this flood of students they are not supposed to have.

Essentially the choice in the future is whether the regular student wants to come to a face-to-face lecture with material projected from a computer or whether he or she wants to see the video and audio clips prepared by the lecturer through the web or on videotape. The number of in class lecture hours for a course will go down as the real discussion moves online. The area that needs considerable rethinking is the budget allocation process and the associated role of distance learning.

The view of the distance learning office is usually that their objective is the service of the remote student. We are entering a world where students need the flexibility of determining when they are remote and when they are not. A clear distinction will be hard to maintain and gradually become meaningless. There are many aspects where the distance learning program has significant impact on the regular program. For example, the presence of videos of class lectures in the library has been a significant aid to the regular student who has missed one or more lectures because of sickness or work commitments. It has also proved useful for those with language problems who need to listen more than once to a lecture. However, there is no library mission or budget to provide the tapes of courses for access by regular students. As a result the tape collection availability is a far more limited in hours than the normal hours for the library. The tape library comes out of the distance learning office budget and not out of the library.

When we talk about software to support this area we talk about communication protocols and human roles built into the software to aid the instructor in promoting equal participation and facilitate the communication process. We see an instructor as having a mental model of complex problem solving in that domain and trying to convey to the students the structure of that model and how to adapt their thinking process to learn and integrate that model. Whether it be engineering design, computer programming, literary analysis, historical understandings of events, or whatever, it is still that fundamental endeavor. When we talk about advanced software in this area we talk about Collaborative Semantic Hypertext templates that the instructor can design to allow an intense discussion to be come self organizing.

We see many instances where the interpretation of the use of communications is to have a faculty member present taped lectures and have a graduate student or staff person conduct question - answer conferences with no attempt at collaboration and no real involvement of the actual faculty member to facilitate and guide the students.

Challenges of Distance Learning

Distance learning faces challenges from facotors of such as:

— Maximum number of students

— Minimum costs

— Course multimedia notes and assignments for use on the web.

— Multimedia material includes video and audio clips to replace lecture.

— Animation to replace derivation type instruction.

— Teaching assistant (student, staff) to answer questions by individual students.

— Adjunct faculty or staff to back up what TA can't handle.

— Third level in hierarchy might actually be person running course and appearing on video clips but only to handle unusual problems.

— CAI and other software to allow the student to conduct skill building exercises.

— No group but individual students repeating an automated version of the correspondence course.

— with one TA for every 50 students we can have unlimited number of students in a single offering.

— Students can start at any time and end at any time and a course becomes continuous operation.

There is really nothing wrong with any of the components to the darkside when they are used appropriately to develop skills and in effect offer training to the student. There are software systems that can check for good coding so that an instructor does not have to spend his or her time reading and checking every program written by a student. But they will not teach a student the pragmatics of how to decompose a particular application for a program design except for essentially trivial examples. The advantage of automation for skills is that it can free the faculty to teach the stuff that cannot be automated. Once a body of subject material is so well understood can be delivered by the Darkside it will probably be offered quite cheaply as a commercial software package presented as a product in training and/ or self learning. At this point the material is probably no longer worthy of what students in the future will expect of a university education. This future may take twenty or thirty years but it will come.

Accreditation of Distance Learning

In US, The Middle States Association of Colleges and Schools recently issued, via the Commission on Higher Education, a policy statement on Distance Learning. This is a very significant document that if taken seriously and if enforced will go a long way to improving the current situation with distance learning in the U.S. Until now accreditation reviews have paid little attention to what was going on in this area. One suspects that, until recently, the common administration view of distance education was that it was a source of revenue. If one could offer distance courses at higher costs to the students, provide less in administrative costs, and also utilize adjuncts to provide most of the courses, the results would be a significant profit generating operation. By organizing it as a separate administration unit the usual department and faculty quality controls could be avoided or minimized. The Middle States document appears to recognize fully that the "use of information and distributed technologies has also allowed institutions to develop innovative instructional methodologies that enhance and complement learning in the traditional classroom environment." However they are still one step away from recognizing that those same technologies can completely remove the distinction between distance learning and normal classroom learning. What they do recognize is:

> "Educational programs conducted off campus, or special programs offered on-campus, must meet standards comparable to those of all other institutional offerings."

What is significant is the interpretation of the above guideline in this new document and we will only select out some items specific to this discussion:

The institution's programs holding specialized accreditation meet the same requirements when offered electronically.

Clearly this means there should be no distinction on inputs or outputs associated with either program and that integration is one desirable approach to accomplishing this.

Qualified faculty provide appropriate oversight of the program electronically offered. This is specific that is needed as general policy through out higher education. This is defied in any situation where administrators choose adjuncts and where there is no responsibility of a faculty member to oversee or mentor a course taught by an adjunct. This should apply to regular courses as well.

The program provides faculty support services specifically related to teaching via an electronic system . The program provides training for faculty who teach via the use of the technology.

In these times of tightening budgets the new common administrative view is that faculty should start buying their own equipment. However, this does not solve the need for specialized peripheral equipment to handle graphics, drawings, digitization, and multimedia (video and audio recordings) that needs to be provided in a multimedia lab environment where faculty can process their own materials. A true multimedia workstation with adequate peripheral equipment is still in the seven to ten thousand dollar range.

The program provides for appropriate real-time or delayed interaction between faculty and students and among students. It is a pleasure to see a realization that electronic mail is no longer considered sufficient and that some sort of group communication processes will evidently be required.

Enrolled students have reasonable and adequate access to the range of student services to support their learning. Many institutions have significant auxiliary services such as tutoring, counseling, librarians, etc. that are not yet provided to the distance students. For example, in a recent case of potential cheating the Dean of Students offices was at a loss as how to hold a formal hearing (as required) when a distance student was involved.

Policies for faculty evaluation include appropriate consideration of teaching and scholarly activities related to electronically offered programs. Here is the crux of a trend that will change the nature of college education. Adjuncts and staff are not going to receive the resources and time to engage in scholarly activities. Their knowledge of any field that is in evolving is going to deteriorate over time and so is their ability to teach timely material or undertake curriculum development activities.

The institution evaluates the program's educational effectiveness, including assessments of student learning outcomes, student retention, and student and faculty satisfaction. Students have access to such program evaluation data. The institution provides for assessment and document of student achievement in each course and at completion of the program.

Certainly the evaluation data on individual courses, programs, and faculty is NOT available to students. In the Virtual Classroom area they can find it in the nature of research reports, publications and books but they are not likely to know where to look. At some universities the evaluation of courses is done by students and published in the student newspapers. Ultimately there will be commercial offerings of course by course evaluations by outside organizations via the web. Once again this is the issue of academic oversight or mentoring of any offerings by adjuncts. If accreditation agencies are going to take their guidelines seriously they need to start requiring review of the resumes of all the adjuncts being used in an academic program and not merely focus on easy measures such as the percentage of use. There is nothing wrong with using a higher percentage if the adjuncts have appropriate backgrounds and they are mentored appropriately by regular faculty who get proper credit for doing this function. Formal faculty review of adjuncts and other non faculty teachers is not currently a uniform institutional practice.

A decent computer conferencing system is required if collaborative learning is an explicit objective of the program. It is this area that truly leads to the realization that an institution cannot teach a subject one way to its regular students and choose to offer a completely different alternative to the distance students. The accreditation problem would be better served if the accreditation agencies realized that the root of the problem is that they should be accrediting the educators as well as the programs. As more and more courses come on to the web it is going to become difficult for consumers to realize what they are getting for their money. There are already courses in creative writing, poetry and other such subjects offered by private individuals over the web. There are a growing number of technical courses being offered by companies and covering, in theory, the same skills offered in university based courses. Most of these are cheaper than their university counterparts. Once can also expect nationwide tutoring services by companies and individuals quite similar to what has happened with the entrance exam coaching operations.

Two other interesting items that probably also generate some controversy from administrators and which did not appear in the final document were:

— policies addressing teaching load, class size, time needed for course conversion/development, and the sharing of instructional responsibilities should be reviewed.

— one of the consistent responsibilities of faculty continues to be the development and oversight of an institution's academic programs.

Trying to shoehorn the current policies into the new technology is a common approach that does not work and discourages beneficial use of the technology. Those, like NJIT, having had grants that covered some the associated conversion and development costs, had been at an advantage many other institutions will not have. But the need for improved workload policies still remains an issue that will end up as part of the labor-management negotiation process. There is a confusion at many institutions between faculty governance and union authority in a number of these areas. As a result administrations may have more power than they should have to dictate in these areas. Also as a result of financial cutbacks there has been a trend for administrations to ignore or sidestep faculty oversight.

Perhaps one of the major issues facing both providers and recipients of electronically offered distance learning programs is achieving parity with traditional on-campus courses. Starting with such a view becomes a self-fulfilling prophecy as one will then design a system that is actually inferior. By incorporating the Virtual Classroom and collaborative learning in traditional courses, those traditional courses are far better than any normal traditional course.

Students must be able to get departmental advisement, deal with the registrar, the library, the bursar, the tutoring center, the student dean and all the other normal on campus functions. Many of these offices do not provide web based access to these services. If they did, a great many regular students would also utilize this approach since it is far more efficient for the student than the phone or having to come to campus to handle a problem. This problem also results from the concept that the distance students are separate from the on campus students and that the distance learning office should be the only interface to the distance student. This view is really inadequate. For most services the distinction made between Distance Learning and on campus students should disappear. There is little doubt at this point that the technologies being employed for the distance students are or could be a boon to the improvement of the quality of education for the on campus students. Using conferencing based systems for regular face to face classes makes a significant improvement in the learning process if the instructor has the right training and attitudinal skills to employ the technology. Furthermore, it is only possible to get the synergy of a classroom atmosphere in the conferencing technology with a critical mass of active students, such as 15 or more. Integrating distance students into regular classes another is also a way to be able to support small numbers of distance students who are interested in specialized electives without large student audiences. The technology may very well make more diverse course offerings economically feasible.

The distinction between distance students and regular students will disappear in that local students will select when they wish to take a course via electronic technology or via the physical classroom. Another option that is also feasible is that some courses can get along with fewer hours of lecture during the week given the sizable on line discussion and assignment activities in the conferencing environment.

A three semester system for Institutions of higher learning would be an extremely desirable situation for distance courses. It would also carry considerable appeal for faculty and students who could choose to take their "summers" during any one of the three semesters. In the new environment where a majority of students are working full time and/or have families, the concept of three equal semesters a year has many desirable qualities. On the other hand the four quarter system probably leads to a too compressed time scale for asynchronous communication oriented courses. This latter point is an intuitive conjecture that could bear closer examination. Those now doing remote classes in the summer usually choose to do it over the two separate summer sessions that NJIT now offers. Most institutions need improved tracking and measurement systems to truly track performance type measures such as throughput times for degrees and more comparative information about student performance correlated with types of instructional delivery and programs. It is amazing how little data is available in this era of institutions gloating over how highly computerized and modernized they have become.

The networking technology for distance education is opening up all universities and colleges to competition. Students can now cross geographical barriers and take courses in any state, or for that matter, any country. The current growing cost of higher education and the trend to cutbacks of public support in the U.S. is forcing many students to put costs first in seeking an education and to act as consumers in a market economy. Universities need to publish better pragmatic data on things like throughput rates or related job performance of their graduates. If faculty and the institutions they represent do not take the initiative to provide evaluative data for the benefit of the perspective students than others will.

Effectiveness of Distance Learning

Distance learning is not a new phenomenon. With the development of the postal service in the 19 th century, commercial correspondence colleges provided distance education to students across the country. This trend continued well into the 20 th century with the advent of radio, television, and othᵉr media that allowed for learning at a distance. In the last decade, providing education at a distance has changed significantly as the use of computer-mediated learning, two-way interactive video, and other technologies has increased. Many universities are making substantial investments in new technologies for teaching. What impact is all of this technology having on the educational effectiveness of colleges and universities? Professor of engineering and applied science at the University of Virginia, makes the following observation about this issue:

> "Universities are in the information business, and technological developments are transforming that industry. University professors from a variety of disciplines have helped create the technologies that are forcing many U.S. industries to reinvent themselves, have advised industry leaders on how to adapt, and have analyzed the importance of changes for society. But it is harder to look inward to the university and to think about whether it might change in dramatic ways."

In recent years, colleges and universities have spent a great deal of time and effort in looking inward to analyze the efficacy of learning through the use of technology. This includes policy papers, "how to" articles, and essays, as well as a limited, though not insignificant body of original research. With few exceptions, the bulk of these writings suggests that the learning outcomes of students using technology at a distance are similar to the learning outcomes of students who participate in conventional classroom instruction. The attitudes and satisfaction of students using distance learning also are characterized as generally positive.

There is no question that there is an impressive amount of writing that concludes that distance learning is viable and effective. The purpose of this analysis is to examine the research more closely so that public policy may be better informed. What are the findings of the research on the effectiveness of distance education? Are they valid? Are there gaps in the research that require further investigation and information? What does the literature suggest for the future? These questions are becoming more and more important as pressure grows-both from within and outside the academy-to use technology as a primary method for delivering higher education. To explore these issues in more detail, the American Federation of Teachers and the National Education Association commissioned The Institute for Higher Education Policy to conduct a review of the research on distance education.

— Reviews the findings of the original research and assesses the overall quality of the analysis;

— Identifies gaps or omissions in the body of original research; and

— Discusses the implications of the research.

Because of the large amount of information available, the scope of this review is limited to written material published during the 1990s. Particular attention is focused on those types of technologies currently being used by the majority of institutions, as identified in a 1997 study by the National Center for Education Statistics (NCES). They include two-way interactive video, one-way prerecorded video, two-way audio/one-way video, and computer-mediated learning. It is important to understand what is meant by distance learning. Because the technology is evolving, the definition of what distance learning is continues to change. Distance learning generally includes synchronous communication, which occurs when teacher and student are present at the same time during instruction-even if they are in two different places-and asynchronous communication, which occurs when students and teachers do not have person-to-person direct interaction at the same time or place.

According to a recent report by the Council for Higher Education Accreditation, distance learning also is characterized by several key factors. Among the most important are that the teaching/learning process involves activities where the learners are at a distance from the originator of the teaching material, and that a combination of media-including television, videotapes, audiotapes, videoconferencing, audioconferencing, e-mail, telephone, fax, Internet, computer software, and print-may be used.

Analytic Approach

While this review of original research does not encompass every study published since 1990, it does capture the most important and salient of these works. The analysis includes over 40 of these original works of research. In addition, several hundred articles, essays, and other writings published in major journals on distance learning have been collected. These other essays, narratives, and reviews of older research are helpful, but do not provide sufficient evidence to accurately assess the effectiveness of distance learning. This paper therefore concentrates primarily on an evaluation of the original research, and summarizes the key information and findings of the non-original research writings. The original research utilizes various approaches, including: descriptive research; case studies; correlational research; and experimental research. The overwhelming majority of research studies used one or more of these types of designs.

Descriptive research involves the collection of data to answer specific questions. Data are usually collected through questionnaires, interviews, or standardized attitude scales. An important component of descriptive research is the validation of the questionnaire in order to determine if it measures what it was developed to measure. Data also can be collected through observation, for instance, analyzing student grades. In distance learning, typical descriptive studies are concerned with the assessment of attitudes, opinions, and conditions. The researcher can use a variety of methods to gather data, however, the explanation of the unit is generally written in narrative form. In distance learning, the case study usually involves a class of students taking a course through some type of electronic means.

Correlational research involves collecting data in order to determine whether, and to what degree, a relationship exists between two or more quantifiable variables. An estimate is provided of just how related two variables are. If two variables are highly related, a correlation coefficient near +1.00 (or -1.00) will be obtained; if two variables are not related, a coefficient near .00 will be obtained. It is important to note that correlational research never establishes a cause-effect relationship. One example of a correlational study might be determining the relationship (correlation) between student satisfaction with an instructor and the type of technology used.

Experimental research is the only type of research that can truly test hypotheses concerning cause- and-effect relationships. In an experimental study, the researcher manipulates at least one independent variable and observes the effect on one or more dependent variables. In other words, the researcher determines "who gets what," which group of subjects will get which treatment. The groups are generally referred to as experimental and control groups. Ideally, in experimental research the groups to be studied are randomly formed before the experiment, a procedure not involved in other methods of research. The essence of experimentation is the notion of control. The researcher strives to insure that the experiences of the groups are as equal as possible on all important variables except the independent variable. In a study of distance education, a good example is comparing one group of students receiving instruction in a traditional classroom (the control group) with another group of students receiving instruction through two-way interactive video. It should be emphasized that the review provided striking evidence of the fact that there is a relative paucity of true, original research dedicated to explaining or predicting phenomena related to distance learning.

The more limited group of original research on the effectiveness of distance learning addresses a variety of issues. Three broad measures of the effectiveness of distance education are usually examined in the original research. These include:

— Student outcomes, such as grades and test scores;

— Student attitudes about learning through distance education; and E Overall stûdent satisfaction toward distance learning.

Most of these studies conclude that, regardless of the technology used, distance learning courses compare favorably with classroom-based instruction and enjoy high student satisfaction. Several examples illustrate this point. One study compared student grades and attitudes at the sending site for several two-way interactive video courses with student grades and attitudes at the receiving site. The courses included education, nursing, and philosophy. Students at the receiving site attained lower grades than the students at the sending site. On the other hand, receiving site students in general portrayed a more positive attitude than sending site students.

Another study compared the results of a take-home essay exam for students who participated in a live broadcast televised graduate course in management of technology with the results for students in the on-campus classroom. The students participating in distance learning performed better than students in the conventional classroom and had less inter-student variation. Term papers for the groups also were compared and no significant difference was found. With respect to homework, the distance learning students performed at a higher level.

At the high school level, a study compared the attitudes and achievements scores of students participating in an anatomy and physiology course taught in a regular classroom and delivered through interactive satellite. No significant differences were found between the attitudes of either group toward the courses. However, the group taught via satellite had higher mean scores on an achievement test than students in the classroom. In one study, students who registered for a Sociology 101 course on campus were told that the course instead would be taught by a one-way televised broadcast. The group's performance with respect to attrition and grades was then compared to another group of students from the community who took the same course, also via one-way televised broadcast, but in their homes, not in a classroom on campus. Both sections experienced a high percentage of students who did not complete the course (44 percent of the on-campus students, and 33 percent of the "off-campus" students).

The off-campus students had much higher grades than the on-campus students, although both groups rated the course as good or excellent. A higher proportion of on-campus students reported that they would not recommend the telecourse to a friend. Another study compared three groups of teachers participating in an in-service microcomputer applications training course: one group was taught by computer-mediated learning, another group of teachers was taught on campus, and yet another group was taught through correspondence. The outcomes measured included scores on achievement tests, time-on-task, student attitudes, and dropout rates. While the results were mixed, the scores on achievement tests were highest for students taking a correspondence course and lowest for students participating in computer-mediated learning. The computer-mediated learning and correspondence students spent more time-on-task than the on-campus students.

Furthermore, there was a significant difference in the attitudes of students; the computer-mediated learning group was less positive toward the course than the conventional classroom group. These examples of experimental research are consistent with many other studies that indicate students participating in distance learning courses perform as well as their counterparts in a traditional classroom setting. The research suggests that there is no difference in student performance does not mean that distance learning is necessarily better than other methods of learning, just that it can be as effective.

There is also a body of descriptive analysis and case studies that focuses on student and faculty attitudes and perceptions of distance learning. The purpose of many of these types of research is to develop recommendations to improve distance learning. One such study examined the perceptions and attitudes of students and faculty toward computer-mediated learning and courses broadcast over a local television channel. A majority of faculty observed that the distance learning students were "more serious, accomplished, and articulate" compared to on-cam-pus students. The distance learning students also had stronger analytical skills and written communication skills, and were more "self-directed" than their on-campus counterparts. The students reported that they chose distance education because of the flexible schedule, and nearly half of the students noted that the instructional method also influenced their decision. Students preferred not to commute and "enjoyed the luxury of not having to commit to a specific class meeting time." Approximately 40 percent of the students reported missing the face-to-face interactions and one-fourth missed the group dynamics. One of the major recommendations of this study was to "explore alternative ways to meet students' interaction needs" on a continuous basis. Several conclusions can be drawn from research that examined courses offered to U.S. Army and Navy personnel through two-way interactive video. These conclusions include: the choice of technology influences the instructional design; origination and remote site technicians are crucial; adequate training for staff is necessary; sufficient practice and technical support are necessary because personnel are often intimidated by new technology; and activities need to be designed to allow students to interact with each other.

In another descriptive study involving two-way interactive video, graduate nursing students were surveyed about their satisfaction regarding the technology. The majority of the respondents were very positive concerning distance education and requested more distance learning opportunities. There was, however, considerable dissatisfaction with the accessibility of the library. Graduate education students participated in another study to determine their perceptions of two-way interactive video courses. Using written surveys, interviews, and class observations, the authors reported very mixed reactions from the students, which resulted in several specific recommendations.

In addition to recommending that the audio quality needed to be improved, it was suggested that future training programs include information on successful strategies for instruction and use more graphics. A toll-free phone number was proposed to contact the instructor. One final example from the original research is a study that attempted to identify specific student attributes associated with student success in computer-mediated learning. Student success was defined as whether newly enrolled students passed their first course using computer-mediated learning. The following student characteristics were identified as being correlated with success.

— Students who rated themselves highly on various measures of persistence related to taking on new projects;

— Married students;

— Students who rated the consequences of not passing as serious;

— Students who rated their chances of succeeding in their studies higher than non-completers;

— Students who did not need support from others to complete difficult tasks and did not find it important to discuss course work with other students;

— Students with high literacy levels;

— Students who rated themselves as well organized in terms of time management skills and said they generally had the time to do what they intended to do;

— Students who rated their formal and informal learning as high in terms of preparing them for university studies; and Female students.

In sum, many experimental studies conclude that students participating in distance learning courses perform as well as their counterparts in a traditional classroom setting. These studies suggest that the distance learning students have similar grades or test scores, or have the same attitudes toward the course. The descriptive analysis and case studies focus on student and faculty attitudes and perceptions of distance learning. The purpose of many of these types of research is to develop recommendations to improve distance learning. These studies typically conclude that students and faculty have a positive view toward distance learning. A closer look at the research, however, reveals that it may not be prudent to accept these findings at face value.

In examining the more limited group of original research, several problems with the conclusions reached through the research are apparent. The most important problem is that the overall quality of the original research is questionable and thereby renders many of the findings inconclusive. The findings of the original research must be read with some caution. Assessing the quality of the original research requires a determination that the studies adhered to commonly accepted principles of good research. The analysis is much more than an academic exercise. These principles are essential if the results of the studies are to be considered valid and generalizable. If a study does not abide by these principles, the results can be erroneous or misleading, and therefore lead to conclusions that result in poor public policy.

The analysis revealed several methodological flaws that should give pause to an objective observer. This is not necessarily surprising. Merely being published in a journal or book, for example, does not guarantee the quality of the study or that it was reported accurately. For instance, in a study which involved a meta-analysis of interactive video instruction, 367 experimental or quasi-experimental studies initially were identified for consideration. However, only 63 studies (17 percent) were chosen for the analysis because the remaining studies had methodological flaws, such as small sample size, high subject mortality, or the lack of minimal data to compute effect size (including means, standard deviations, t test, and F values). Unfortunately, many of these same criticisms apply to the research reviewed for this paper.

The following are the key shortcomings of the original research on the effectiveness of distance learning. Much of the research does not control for extraneous variables and therefore cannot show cause and effect. Lack of control for extraneous variables is a major shortcoming that pertains particularly to experimental research, where the researcher attempts to compare the outcomes of a control group with the outcomes of an experimental group. Most experimental studies of distance learning are designed to measure how a specific technology—the "cause"-impacts upon some type of learning outcome or influences the attitudes of students-the "effect." To accurately assess this relationship, other potential "causes" must not influence the measured outcomes. If other variables influence outcomes, it is impossible to attribute "cause" to the technology being used.

In almost all of the experimental research reviewed for this paper, there was inadequate control of extraneous variables. This analysis is consistent with a 1992 inquiry of 150 articles and studies that compared distance education learning to conventional classroom instruction, which found that differences other than the technology "could not be ruled out as key causal agents." One example involves a study comparing students taking a statistics class in a traditional classroom and through computer-mediated learning.

Lack of random selection of subjects is closely aligned with control of extraneous variables, and is another major weakness in the research evaluating distance learning. The single best way of controlling for extraneous variables is to assign students randomly to both the experimental and control groups. Using the previous example, if random selection of subjects was used, it would be expected that the students would be similar with respect to motivation, experience, age, etc. However, many of the published studies reviewed used intact groups for comparison purposes. As a result, these studies run the risk of having a number of variables affecting academic achievement or student satisfaction, not just the technology used to provide education at a distance.

One important caveat: random selection does not guarantee that the control and experimental groups are similar in all attributes, but it is an accepted practice in good research and is considerably better than using intact groups. In addition, it should be noted that while there are statistical procedures for pretesting that can be utilized if intact groups are used, in many studies these procedures were not employed. An important component of good educational research relates to proper measurement of learning outcomes and/or student attitudes. In short, do the instruments-such as final examinations, quizzes, questionnaires, or attitude scales-measure what they are supposed to measure? A well-conducted study would include the validity and reliability of the instruments so that the reader can have confidence in the results. In almost all of the studies reviewed, this information was lacking. Not only were the data regarding the appropriateness of the instruments absent, it was clear that the validity and reliability of the tests or questionnaires were not even determined. In a study assessing students' initial perceptions of distance learning, the author developed a survey based upon other surveys targeting course satisfaction. There was no evidence that the survey used pilot testing or other techniques to enhance validity.

Many other studies involved the use of teacher produced examinations, which have not followed established methods for ensuring high levels of validity and reliability. It is rare to find a teacher-made test in the research that is based upon persuasive evidence of content or construct validity. Many studies do not adequately control for the feelings and attitudes of the students and faculty-what the educational research refers to as "reactive effects." Reactive effects are a number of factors associated with the way in which a study is conducted and the feelings and attitudes of the students involved. Two are worth mentioning here because they were evident in many of the studies under review. One reactive effect, known as the Novelty Effect, refers to increased interest, motivation, or participation on the part of students simply because they are doing something different, not better per se.

Another, called the John Henry Effect, refers to control groups or their teachers feeling threatened or challenged by being in competition with a new program or approach and, as a result, outdoing themselves and performing well beyond what normally would be expected. When this effect occurs, the experimental treatment may not appear to be very effective. The Novelty Effect in particular can be observed when distance learning is used for the first time. In one case study, the first offering of a distance learning course was investigated. Using a variety of observational methods, the attitudes of both students and faculty regarding the delivery mode and methods of instruction were ascertained. Since the students and faculty were keenly aware of this new venture, their responses needed to be analyzed with some level of reservation.

A significant portion of the research reviewed possesses serious weaknesses that call into question their results. That is not to say that well-constructed research designs were not found in the literature. Indeed, studies were found that provided the reader with some confidence in the findings. Unfortunately, they were in the minority. Moore and his colleagues make this point plainly in their review of the literature on distance learning's effectiveness.

The weight of evidence that can be gathered from the literature points overwhelmingly to the conclusion that teaching and studying at a distance, especially that which uses interactive electronic telecommunications media, is effective, when effectiveness is measured by the achievement of learning, by the attitudes of students and teachers, and by cost effectiveness. It is necessary to append several reservations to this optimistic conclusion. The sheer weight of opinion in the literature should not be taken as conclusive of itself, since most of it is based on anecdotal evidence offered by persons and institutions with vested interests in the techniques being evaluated, or in the very programs they are evaluating. Furthermore, in those studies where some attempt has been made to gather empirical data, the research has been undertaken by schoolteachers or university faculty with extremely limited resources. As a result, the methodology of many of the research designs is weak, with regard to such factors as the populations being compared or otherwise studied; the treatments being given, the statistical techniques being applied, and the validity, reliability, and generalizability of the data on which the conclusions are based.

Notwithstanding the fact that the overall quality of the research needs improvement, there are several important issues regarding the effectiveness of distance learning that require further investigation and information. These gaps must be filled so that public policy discussions are based on accurate and adequate information. The discussion below identifies those areas of research that either need to be strengthened or are absent from the literature. The research has tended to emphasize student outcomes for individual courses rather than for a total academic program. A major gap in the research is the lack of studies dedicated to measuring the effectiveness of total academic programs taught using distance learning. Virtually all of the comparative or descriptive studies focus upon individual courses. This raises important questions about whether a total program delivered by technology compares favorably with a program provided on campus. Many institutions advertise that students can complete a degree without leaving their home by participating in distance learning in a number of ways, including computer-mediated learning, receiving videotapes, or watching courses through their local cable network.

The overall impact of a college education, particularly the baccalaureate degree, is of considerable concern to educators, the general public, and public policy leaders alike. A college education is intended to impart much more than an accumulation of facts. The seminal study How College Affects Students, by Pascarella and Terenzini, provides an excellent summary of the outcomes of an undergraduate degree. In addition to certain cognitive skills and verbal, quantitative, and subject matter competence, the authors identify several other outcomes of students who complete a college degree. They include psychosocial changes, such as identity, self-concept, self-esteem, and relating to others in the external world; advancement of critical thinking skills; development of attitudes and values; moral development; and career choice and development. To the extent that these attributes are important, an entire body of research needs to be developed to determine if students participating in distance learning for their whole program compare favorably with students taught in the conventional classroom. To be sure, researchers tend to measure what they can measure. Conducting such research would take an enormous commitment of both time and money, let alone finding an adequate sample.

On the other hand, this issue strikes at the very core of what a college education is all about and the degree to which distance education students benefit. The research does not take into account differences among students. A substantial portion of research on distance learning has been conducted to demonstrate no significant difference in achievement levels between groups of distance and traditional learners. However, there is wide variance of achievement and attitudes within the groups, which indicates that learners have a variety of different characteristics. The factors influencing these differences could include gender, age, educational experience, motivation, and others. Gathering samples of students and amalgamating them into averages produces an illusory "typical learner," which masks the enormous variability of the student population. Stated more plainly, experimental studies in distance learning are using an "agricultural-botany paradigm-assuming that students react to different educational treatments as consistently as plants react to fertilizers." Further research needs to focus on how individuals learn, rather than how groups learn. This is particularly important because technology has the potential to individualize learning to a greater degree than previously known.

The research does not adequately explain why the dropout rates of distance learners are higher. In a number of studies, there was evidence that a higher percentage of students participating in a distance learning course tended to drop out before the course was completed compared to students in a conventional classroom. For instance, in one study, while the mean pass mark was 81 percent, only 40 percent of the students successfully completed the course. In another study, one-third of the students in a videoconferencing class received the grade of "I" (incomplete), compared to only 15 percent in an on-campus course. In another study comparing an engineering course taught in a conventional classroom to one taught through computer-mediated learning, 95 percent of the resident students finished the course, compared to 64 percent of the computer-mediated learning students. One other study found that students participating in computer-mediated learning had significantly higher incompletion rates (32 percent) than the on-cam-pus students (4 percent). The issue of student persistence (called subject mortality by researchers) is troubling because of both the negative consequences associated with dropping out, and the fact that the research could be excluding these dropouts-thereby tilting the student outcome findings toward those who are "successful." For example, if the average mean score of an achievement test or the score from a survey measuring student satisfaction is based upon a smaller number of students than had registered for the course, the data could be invalid. In other words, if the students who had dropped out had remained in the course, the mean score of the achievement test or student survey could be significantly different.

A major reason for providing distance education is to provide access to students who normally would not be able to participate in higher education. If a substantial number of students fail to complete their courses, the notion of access becomes meaningless. Distance learning studies should clearly indicate the beginning and ending number of students in a course to ensure that dropouts are not excluded from the analysis. The research does not take into consideration how the different learning styles of students relate to the use of particular technologies. Similar to the relationship of course content and technology, understanding of how the learner, the learning task, and a particular technology interact is limited. Learner characteristics are a major factor in the achievement and satisfaction levels of the distance learner.

Information regarding a student's preferred learning style will influence how the course is designed and the type of technology to be used. The development of software could be enhanced from a better understanding of the properties of technology (such as interactive and passive characteristics) with factors such as complexities of tasks, and cognitive, affective, and psychomotor skills. Additional research could result in more information regarding why different technologies might be better suited for specific learning tasks. In one study that attempted to address these issues, students were self-assigned to two groups: an on-campus conventional class, and a remote distance learning class using two-way interactive video. The students were administered the Canfield Learning Styles Inventory to ascertain each student's primary learning style. The author concluded that learning style preferences may affect academic achievement and attitudes of students participating in distance learning. However, the study has limited validity because of a small number of subjects, all of which were female.

The research focuses mostly on the impact of individual technologies rather than on the interaction of multiple technologies. Much of the literature on distance learning focuses on one technology and either describes its effectiveness and/or compares it to the conventional classroom experience. Practitioners in the field are learning that most technologies are multifunctional and can be adapted to address a wide range of learning outcomes. Using a combination of technologies is now being labeled the "third generation" of distance learning systems (the first and second being correspondence courses and the current use of single mediums, respectively). For instance, combining two-way interactive video with computer-mediated learning could prove to be a very powerful tool for learning, particularly higher order thinking skills.

The third generation models often use a combination of print, videotape, audio tape, fax, audio conferencing, and voice mail. Combining these technologies with computer- mediated learning enhances interaction between student and student, and student and teacher. Unfortunately, there are few studies that examine more than one technology-and the synergistic effects of certain technologies-in addressing specific educational outcomes and particular student groups. The few studies that are available do not provide sufficient grounds for generalization because of a range of limitations, including small sample sizes and lack of sufficient explanation of the instructional treatment. The research does not include a theoretical or conceptual framework. There is a vital need to develop a more integrated, coherent, and sophisticated program of research on distance learning that is based on theory. Theories serve both as goals and tools-as means and ends. As goals, they provide explanations for specific phenomenon with maximal probability. As tools, they provide an underlying framework for observation and discovery by governing the kind of phenomena that investigators study.

Theory allows researchers to build on the work of others and, increase the probability of addressing the more significant questions regarding distance learning. Using theory as a guiding framework also allows the research to be replicated and enhances its generalizability, therefore making individual studies more meaningful. Several authors have lamented that there are no theories that deal with the interactions and interrelationships of variables in terms of the effectiveness of distance learning programs. The research does not adequately address the effectiveness of digital "libraries." Students participating in distance learning, particularly those in remote locations, are often introduced to a digital "library" that provides access to bibliographies, as well as full-text, of a variety of resources. The library is at the core of the higher education experience and, especially at the graduate level, is an integral part of the teaching/learning process. Some digital libraries boast an enormous array of resources, with the implicit notion that they can provide the same service as the traditional library. There is some concern, however, that these showcase libraries are not representative of other digital libraries.

Implications

Research on distance learning has been driven by what many are calling the "information revolution." The rapid evolution and advances in technology offer both the general public and faculty a dizzying array of challenges that are unprecedented. For the last four decades, the speed and storage capacity of computers have doubled every 18-24 months; the cost, size, and power consumption have become smaller at about the same rate. The bandwidth of computer networks has increased a thousandfold in just the last decade, and the traffic on the network continues to grow at 300-500 percent annually. For the foreseeable future, all of these trends will continue; the basic technology to support their continued advance exists now. Technology is having, and will continue to have, a profound impact on colleges and universities in America and around the globe. Distance learning, which was once a poor and often unwelcome stepchild within the academic community, is becoming increasingly more visible as a part of the higher education family. But the research and literature reviewed for this paper indicate that the higher education community has a lot to learn regarding how, and in what ways, technology can enhance the teaching/learning process, particularly at a distance. As with other educational innovations that have come before it, there is some danger that the innovations made possible through distance education are advancing more rapidly than our understanding of its practical uses. The electronic publishing has passed through three stages since its inception in the 1940s: "an initial phase of utopian enthusiasm, a period of disillusionment, and a new tendency toward pragmatism."

In the context of the research on distance learning and its effectiveness, more emphasis has been placed on the "utopian" possibilities of the technology and its potential to do as well as classroom-based instruction. But not enough "pragmatism" has been applied to allow for a discussion of distance learning's practical implications as a supplement to enhance teaching and learning. There are at least three broad implications that can be derived from this review of the original research and the other literature. The first is that the notion of "access to college" in the distance learning context is unclear. Many of the advocates of distance learning tout access to college-level education as a *raison d'etre* for the proliferation of distance education. Indeed, in some states, public policy leaders are recommending using distance education in lieu of "bricks and mortar" learning. Of particular concern is access as it relates to the efficacy of computer-mediated learning. Unlike two-way interactive video, where students and the instructor can see and talk to each other in a conventional classroom, computer-mediated learning requires special skills of students and more sophisticated technical support if students are to interact fully.

The faculty role will change from being mainly a content expert ('the professor's job is to profess') to a combination of content expert, learning process design expert, and process implementation manager. Faculty also will be motivators and mentors, interpreters (especially of non-codified knowledge), and, as a colleague recently put it, 'expert learners'-people who lead the learning process by breaking the trail and setting the right personal example. Technology can leverage faculty time, but it cannot replace most human contact without significant quality losses." Third, although the ostensible purpose of much of the research is to ascertain how technology affects student learning and student satisfaction, many of the results seem to indicate that technology is not nearly as important as other factors, such as learning tasks, learner characteristics, student motivation, and the instructor. The irony is that the bulk of the research on technology ends up addressing an activity that is fundamental to the academy, namely pedagogy-the art of teaching. To that extent, the research has had a salutary effect in that a rising tide lifts all boats. Any discussion about enhancing the teaching/learning process through technology also has the beneficial effect of improving how students are taught on campus.

Consider this example. In 1987 the American Association of Higher Education (AAHE) published "Seven Principles for Good Practice in Undergraduate Education," which distilled findings from the research on the undergraduate experience. The principles were revived in 1996 to enable those using new communication and information technologies to enhance the teaching/learning process. In one form or another, the principles have been incorporated in a variety of publications on good practice, and were replete in many of the studies. AAHE's Principles for Good Practice in Undergraduate Education include those methods that:

— encourage contacts between students and faculty;

— develop reciprocity and cooperation among students;

— use active learning techniques;

— give prompt feedback;

— emphasize time-on-task;

— communicate high expectations; and

— respect diverse talents and ways of learning.

In a sense, the discussion has come full circle. The research on distance learning has a long way to go, and much of it is inconclusive. On the other hand, technology has helped the academy to continue its focus on the essential goals of teaching and learning.

Bibliography

Anderson, D. T., Garrison, D.R., 1995, "Transactional Issues in Distance Education: The Impact of Design in Audio-conferencing", *American Journal of Distance Education*, 9, 2, pp. 27-45.

Burge, E., 1993, "Adult Distance Learning: Challenges for Contemporary Practice", In Thelma Barer-Stein and James A. Draper (eds.), *The Craft of Teaching Adults*, Toronto, Ontario: Culture Concepts, pp. 131-144.

Comeaux, P., 1995, "The Impact of an Interactive Distance Learning Network on Classroom Communication", *Communication Education*, 41(4), pp. 353-361.

Galusha, J. M., 1998, *Barriers to Learning in Distance Education, Interpersonal Computing and Technology*, 5(3-4), pp. 6-14.

Garrison, D. R., 1990, "An Analysis and Evaluation of Audio Teleconferencing to Facilitate Education at a Distance", *The American journal of Distance Education*, 4, pp. 13-24.

Graham, S.W., and Wedman, J.F., 1989, "Enhancing the Appeal of Teletraining", *Journal of Instructional Psychology*, 16(4), 183-191.

Henri, F., 1992, "Computer Conferencing and Content Analysis", In Kaye, A.R (ed.), *Collaborative Learning through Computer Conferencing*, Springer-Verlag, pp.117.

Jansen, D. G., and Lewis, W. B., 1996, "Creating High-levels of Interaction in Distance Education Courses", *ATEA Journal*, 24(1), pp.8-9.

Kearsley, G., 1995, "The Nature and Value of Interaction in Distance Learning, In M. Koble (ed.), *The American Centre for the Study of Distance Education Invitational Research Conferencing Distance Education: Toward Excellence in Distance Education*, University Park, PA: Penn State University.

Martin, B. L., "Using Distance Education to Teach Instructional Design to Preservice Teachers", *Educational Technology*, Vol. XXXIV, No. 3, March 1994.

McHenry, L., and Bozik, M., 1995, "Communicating at a Distance: A Study of Interaction in a Distance Education Classroom", *Communication Education*, 44(4), pp. 362-371.

Misanchuk, E.R., 1994, "Print Tools in Distance Education", In B. Willis (ed.), *Distance Education: Strategies and Tools*, Englewood Cliffs, NJ: Educational Technology Publications, pp.109-129.

Morgan, A., 1991, *Research into Student Learning in Distance Education*, Victoria, Australia: University of South Australia, Underdale.

Schuemer, R., 1993, *Some Psychological Aspects of Distance Education*, Hagen, Germany: Institute for Research into Distance Education.

Stenerson, F., 1998, "Systems Analysis and Design for a Successful Distance Education Programme Implementation", *Journal of Distance Learning Administration*.

Williams, M., and Paprock, K., 1994, "Instructional Design in Distance Education", *The ED Journal*, 7(4), 1994.

Yucha, C. 8., 1996, Interactive Distance Education: Improvisation helps Bridge the Gap, *Journal of Biocommunication*, 23(1), pp. 2-5.

Index

Academic mission, 6
Accreditation, 268
Administrative costs, 268
America On-Line, 25
Assignment feedback, 3
Asynchronous Learning Networks (ALN), 254
Asynchronous, 22
Audio-visual agenda, 98

Basic skills, 27

Classroom environment, 269
Coaxial cable hybrid system, 45
Commercial networks, 41
Commercial software, 49
Computer network, 26
Computer-assisted instruction, 2
Computer-managed instruction (CMI), 2
Computer-mediated education (CME), 2
Critical media literacy, 161
Culturally multimedia, 111

Democratic literacy, 161
Dependent variables, 280
Digital video editors, 99
Distance Learning, 265

Ecological literacy, 161
Education environment, 18
Education systems, 142
Educational programs, 42
Electronic mail, 61
Extraneous, 286

Front-line teachers, 109

Generic servers, 51
Geographical Information System, 50
Greening, 25
Guest speakers, 25

Hierarchical fashion, 28
Home pages, 29
Hypertext Markup Language (HTML), 29
Hypertext, 28

Informal environment, 145
Information Driveway, 39
Information revolution, 296

Infrastructure, 20
Instructional format, 17
Instructional television (ITV), 66
Instructor's expectations, 5
Interactive Videoconferencing (IV), 73
Internet services, 46
Investigation, 290
Isolation, 40

Learning environment, 27

Management Information Systems, 255
Marginal supplement, 134
Multimedia technologies, 111

National Center for Education Statistics (NCES), 277
Network community, 48
Newtonian schools, 150

Paradigm-assuming, 292
Public policy, 290

Self-preservation, 142
Smart classroom, 22
Student-to-student interaction, 59
Superhighway, 41
Surface approach, 14
Synchronous, 22

Teacher-to-student feedback, 1
Technical requirements, 53
Technological devices, 53
Traditional instruction, 1
Tremendous, 140

Underpinnings, 154
Utopian, 297

Virtual Classroom, 273

Web editors, 52
Web pages, 29
World-Wide Web (WWW), 29